BECOMING
EMOTIONALLY
WHOLE

CHARLES
STANLEY

OLIVER
NELSON

THOMAS NELSON PUBLISHERS
Nashville • Atlanta • London • Vancouver

Published in Nashville, Tennessee, by Thomas Nelson, Inc., Publishers, and distributed in Canada by Word Communications, Ltd., Richmond, British Columbia.

The Bible version used in this publication is THE NEW KING JAMES VERSION. Copyright © 1979, 1980, 1982, Thomas Nelson, Inc., Publishers.

ISBN 0-7852-7275-5

Printed in the United States of America.

CONTENTS

INTRODUCTION

HOW DO YOU FEEL TODAY?

Hｏｗ are you feeling?

We usually ask that question about a person's physical health. It's an equally valid question, however, to ask about a person's emotional state of being.

Each of us has an emotional state of well-being that is just as vital to our overall wholeness as our physical or spiritual well-being. You cannot be a whole person in Christ Jesus if you are in bondage to your emotions or in denial of them.

I continually am amazed at the number of people I meet who try to deny that they have an emotional response to the situations they encounter. They seem to believe that it is weak for a person to cry, a flaw for a person to feel anger or to express disappointment, a lack of self-control for a person to laugh aloud. Such people are missing out on the fullness of what it means to be alive.

An expression of emotion is part of what makes us human. Emotions are a gift of God, who created each of us with a capacity to feel and to express emotions. Furthermore, emotions are vital to our ability to communicate to others the uniqueness of our personalities. They are also a means of responding to God, to other people, and to life in general.

Many people don't know how to express their emotions in healthful ways that promote good relationships with friends and family members. Learning how to deal with one's emotions—how to direct them toward good outcomes, express them without sinning, and give voice to emotions in order to improve communication—is a vital skill.

Still other people allow themselves to have a free-flowing emotional response to life, and they have learned to control their emotions, but they are uncomfortable talking about the way they feel.

Learning how to tell others what you are feeling and why is a part of becoming a mature person. It is a skill that is critical to the development of adult-to-adult relationships.

I don't know where you are today in terms of answering the question "How are you feeling?" I do know this, however: wherever you are on the spectrum of emotional growth—from denial to full expression—the Lord Jesus Christ desires that you have emotional health. He desires that you express emotions in the way that He created them to be expressed. He desires that you freely admit to emotions, that you know how to control them and use them in right ways, and that you discuss your emotional responses with others.

Expressing Emotions

Are there good and bad emotions? Yes and no. Emotions in and of themselves are neutral. Their expression takes on the nature of good and bad.

All emotions are valid. Each has a place in God's design of your human psyche and spirit. God created your emotions so that you might enjoy them, communicate with them.

Each person, to a certain extent, is going to have a unique response to life's situations, problems, circumstances, and challenges. One person may weep at the beauty of a moving piece of music, another person may sit in silent awe, and still another person may stand to give thunderous applause. We must allow others the privilege of their expression.

We also must give one another the privilege of expressing emotions privately. Although I advocate the healthful and free expression of emotions, I do not advocate that a person be required to express emotions in the presence of others.

Conversely, we must be careful not to assume that we have the right to express our emotions freely and fully in the presence of others. Every public expression of emotion should take into consideration the public being asked to witness the emotional display. Simple courtesy and respect should govern our behavior. Restraint is not denial of emotions; it is control of them in the presence of others.

Sometimes we are overcome with emotion. We may lose control in a particular situation or circumstance. At those times, we may feel we should apologize for our lack of control or restraint, but we should never apologize for having feelings. When we apologize for having emotions, we are in danger of stuffing them, with a possible eruption later. Stuffed emotions can be damaging.

Uncharted Waters

For most of us, the realm of emotions has uncharted territories. We are unsure of the language of emotions. We have neglected or feared to explore areas of the inner life.

Recognize at the outset of this study that if this is true for you, it is likely true for every other person you know. Give family members, your circle of friends, other church members, your Bible study group, the freedom to err on their way toward emotional health.

In Summary . . .

God made you to have feelings. He has a desire for you to experience His presence with your emotions, to express yourself emotionally, and to have an emotional relationship with other people.

The Lord desires that you become emotionally whole!

PREPARING FOR A JOURNEY INTO EMOTIONS

This book is intended for Bible study. My hope as you engage in this study is that you will turn again and again to your favorite version of the Bible—to highlight specific words, underline phrases, write in the margins, or circle verses that speak to you in a special way. My Bible is well marked with dates, notes, and insights.

Bookstores are filled with self-help books these days, and many books deal with emotional well-being. The Bible is the ultimate "help" book. The advice that it offers doesn't lead us to self-help, however; rather, it leads us to God's help. The Bible holds God's eternal wisdom about emotions and how we are to express them. Make your Bible your ultimate authority on emotions and how to communicate them.

For Personal or Group Study

You may use this guide on your own or as part of a small-group study. If you use this book for an individual Bible study, you will find many places in which to note key insights or your response to the material presented. If you are using this book for a small-group study, you'll find ample opportunity for discussion.

At various times, you will be asked to identify with the material in one of these ways:

- What new insight have you gained?
- Have you ever had a similar experience?
- How do you feel about the material?
- In what way do you feel challenged to action?

Insights

An insight is seeing something as if it is new to you. It is more than a mere fact or an idea. Most of us have had the experience of reading a passage of the Bible countless times and then one day reading it and saying, "I never noticed that before. I've never seen that truth in all the times I've studied or meditated on these verses." When that happens, you are experiencing a spiritual insight.

Insights can be very personal. Generally speaking, something stands out to us because it relates to us in some way, usually to something we are currently experiencing. At other times, an insight will pull it all together for us. We may have been reading or studying in a certain area for some time when suddenly, we understand more clearly God's meaning or purpose. We have a sudden knowing about what to do, how to think, or why we believe what we believe.

Ask God to give you insights every time you open His Word to read it. I believe He will be faithful in answering your prayer!

As you have insights, make notes about them. If you are intentional about recording your insights, you'll likely find that you have more insights. The more you listen for God to speak to you, the more He does! If you haven't gained new spiritual insights after reading several passages from God's Word, you probably haven't been engaged in the process of study.

From time to time in this guide, you will be asked to note what specific passages of the Bible say to you. This is the time for you to record your personal response, not a group response.

Experiences

Each of us comes to God's Word from a unique background. Each of us has learned about emotions from a unique set of sources. Therefore, each of us has a unique perspective on what is read in God's Word.

What we do have in common are life experiences. We can point to times in which we have found the Bible to be applicable to us—sometimes in a convicting, challenging way, and sometimes in an encouraging, comforting way. We have experiences about which we can say, "I know that truth in the Bible is valid because of what happened to me."

Of course, our experiences do not make the Bible true. The Bible is truth. By noting our experiences, we discover the many ways in which the Bible is applicable to us and to others. We see how God's Word has the potential to speak to every person and to address at some level every situation or circumstance that a person might experience. We discover that God's Word is universal, as well as individual, and that our greatest potential for mutuality, harmony, and unity lies in each of us having a relationship with Christ Jesus and desiring to live according to God's principles.

Sharing experiences is important for spiritual growth. If you are doing this study on your own, I encourage you to talk to others about your faith experiences.

Emotional Responses

This entire book is about emotions, and we have already discussed in the introduction the need to allow others to have their own emotional responses. Very specifically, we need to allow ourselves and others to have emotional responses to God's Word.

Face your emotions honestly. Learn to share them with others.

God expects you to respond to Him and to His Word in an emotional way. Allow yourself to do so, and take note of the way you feel.

When you identify your emotions toward God's Word and what you perceive God is saying to you through His Word, you may be motivated to greater action, or you may have deeper insights into yourself. Both can be means to spiritual growth.

In most small-group settings, I have found it much more beneficial for people to express their emotions than to give their opinions.

Sometimes God speaks to us through His Word in nonverbal ways. His Spirit isn't limited to the words on the page. The Holy Spirit often speaks to us in the unspoken language of intuition, promptings, emotions, and deep desires and longings.

When we share our feelings with one another, we have deeper insights into God's Word, and we also grow closer together as the body of Christ. A sense of community develops, and we understand more clearly what it means to be one in the Spirit. Through the sharing of joys and sorrows, assurances and doubts, we mature not only as individuals, but also as churches.

Challenges

As we read God's Word, we nearly always feel conviction at some point. We feel as if God is speaking directly to us.

The conviction may be about sin in our lives. It may be a clear call to engage in a new behavior or even to pursue a new avenue of ministry or service. It may be a word of correction about a pattern or habit in our lives. I have found in my life that God always challenges me to grow just beyond where I am and to do things that are just beyond my ability to do them. God is never content with the status quo. He is always calling us to grow more like His Son, Jesus Christ.

We need to pinpoint, as best we can, the areas in which we believe God is challenging us—stretching us, molding us, calling us, causing us to believe for more. When we identify what God wants us to do, we are in a better position to take action.

Ultimately, God desires to get His Word into us, and us into His Word, so that we can take His Word into the world, live it out, and be witnesses of His Word in all we say and do. It isn't enough for us to note our insights, recall our experiences, or share our emotions. We must apply what we learn. The Bible challenges us to be doers of His Word and not hearers only (James 1:22).

It isn't enough for you to become personally whole emotionally. You must seek to develop relationships with other people that are marked by emotional maturity and wholeness. You must become an advocate for emotional health and soundness in families, churches, and communities.

Keep the Bible Central

I caution you to keep the Bible at the center of your study. Otherwise, you face the danger of your group becoming a therapy or support group of some type. Therapy and support groups have their time and place, but in the end, it is as we gather around God's Word—to feed upon it, learn from it, and grow into it—that we truly grow spiritually and become all that God created us to be.

If you are doing a personal Bible study, you also must be diligent in staying focused on God's Word. Self-analysis and introspection are not the goals of this study. Growing into the fullness of the stature of Christ Jesus is the goal!

Prayer

Finally, I encourage you to begin and end your Bible study sessions in prayer. Ask God to give you spiritual eyes to see what He wants you to see and spiritual ears to hear what He wants you to hear. Ask Him to give you new insights, to recall to your memory the experiences that are helpful to your growth, and to help you identify your emotions with clarity. Be bold and ask Him to reveal to you in His Word what He desires for you to take as the next step of growth in your spiritual journey.

As you conclude a time of study, ask the Lord to seal to your heart what you have learned so that you will never forget it. Ask Him to transform you more into the likeness of Christ Jesus as you meditate on what you have studied.

The Depths of God's Word

Avoid the temptation of concluding at the end of your ten-week study that you have mastered your emotions. You have probably only begun to explore certain areas of your life. Continue to read God's Word. Continue to grow and to explore what God has to say to you about emotions and all that it means to have a sound mind and heart.

Never stop exploring the riches of God's Word on any topic. I can guarantee you without reservation that if you remain in God's Word on a daily basis, you'll have a much greater understanding about emotional health and wholeness a year from now than you will have at the end of ten weeks. Read God's Word daily. Grow in its truth.

- *What new insights about emotions do you anticipate God may have for you personally?*

  _____

  _____

- *Is there something specific that you hope to gain from this study?*

  _____

  _____

- *In what areas have you struggled with certain emotions in the past?*

  _____

  _____

- *How do you feel about experiencing emotional growth, about expressing emotions more readily, about discussing emotions?*

  _____

  _____

- *Do you feel challenged to grow emotionally as a means of becoming a more effective witness for Christ Jesus?*

  _____

  _____

LESSON 2

GOD CREATED YOUR EMOTIONS

From where do our emotions come? Are they a source of evil or good?

People often ask me these two questions, although not always that directly. At times, people seem to imply that emotions are evil or that it is bad to exhibit certain emotions.

Our emotions are part of our creation. God gave us our emotions. He made us to be emotional creatures.

The first few chapters of the book of Genesis are filled with emotions. In the first chapter, we see that creation arose from God's desire for fellowship with man, the culmination of His creation of the universe. Genesis 2 introduces the concept of loneliness. The Lord says about Adam, "It is not good that man should be alone; I will make him a helper comparable to him" (Gen. 2:18). In the third chapter, we see Adam and Eve experiencing fear. When Adam hears God calling to him, he responds, "I heard Your voice in the garden, and I was afraid because I was naked; and I hid myself" (Gen. 3:10). Desire, loneliness, and fear are three of our most basic emotions, and they appear in the opening verses of the Bible.

• *Identify the last time you felt these emotions:*
Desire (especially a desire to change or to start something new)

_____

_____

Loneliness

_____

_____

Fear

_____

_____

The fruit of the Holy Spirit—the character qualities that the Holy Spirit manifests in our lives—are emotion-laden fruit: love, joy, peace, longsuffering, kindness, goodness, faithfulness, gentleness, and self-control. (See Gal. 5:22–23.) The Holy Spirit has chosen our emotions as His means of expressing Himself in our lives. Conversely, when Paul identifies the works of the flesh, he includes both emotions and behavior.

Take special note of the verses below, and identify areas for growth in your emotional and spiritual life.

What the Word Says

Now the works of the flesh are evident, which are: adultery, fornication, uncleanness, lewdness, idolatry, sorcery, hatred, contentions, jealousies, outbursts of wrath, selfish ambitions, dissensions, heresies, envy, murders, drunkenness, revelries, and the like; of which I tell you before-

What the Word Says to Me

_____

_____

_____

_____

_____

_____

_____

_____

hand, just as I also told you in
time past, that those who prac-
tice such things will not inherit
the kingdom of God. But the
fruit of the Spirit is love, joy,
peace, longsuffering, kindness,
goodness, faithfulness, gentleness, self-control. Against such
there is no law. And those who
are Christ's have crucified the
flesh with its passions and desires. If we live in the Spirit, let
us also walk in the Spirit. Let us
not become conceited, provoking
one another, envying one another (Gal. 5:19–26).

- *In what ways are you feeling challenged to develop greater
  emotional health as part of your spiritual development?*

_____

_____

Let me call your attention specifically to Galatians 5:24: "And
those who are Christ's have crucified the flesh with its passions
and desires." Some people believe this verse implies that we are to
crucify all our passions and desires. That isn't what this verse says.
It says we who are in Christ are to have crucified the *flesh*—in other
words, the fleshly display of passions and desires that Paul terms
"works of the flesh."

Yes, we are to crucify hate, a desire for continual dispute,
jealousy, envy, and the emotions related to selfish ambition and
outbursts of anger. But no, we are *not* to crucify our emotions as a
whole. We have the potential for displaying the Holy Spirit at

work in us through behaviors that rise from love, joy, peace, and so forth.

In a very general sense, our emotions are neutral. They can be turned to good or evil. Our goal as Christians is to control our emotions so that we manifest them in ways that build up others and ourselves.

God would not have given us something inherently bad. That's an important idea to share with someone who believes that her emotions cause her to sin. Emotions can be allowed to run amok to the point that they result in sinful behavior. But the same emotions can also be turned toward Christ and be used to display godly behavior. Our emotions don't get us into trouble. Rather, we sometimes allow our emotions to have free rein over the will, and that gets us into trouble.

Emotions were given to us to *serve* us, not master us.

What Is the Purpose of Our Emotions?

God gave us our emotions for a specific purpose.

The apostle Paul wrote to Timothy these words of encouragement: "For God has not given us a spirit of fear, but of power and of love and of a sound mind" (2 Tim. 1:7). The Lord intends for us to be filled with the power of the Holy Spirit, the emotion of love, and to have the self-control (sound mind) to make wise choices about how we will display the power of the Holy Spirit with love.

Emotions were given to us for very positive reasons, the foremost one of which is to prompt us to act.

We may think that a certain behavior is the right thing to do, but until we feel something with regard to that behavior, we may not act. Take, for example, the person who knows it's dangerous to drive while feeling sleepy. Such a person may think, *I shouldn't drive while I'm so tired.* Still, that person may drive on down the road. But if that person dozes for just a second and awakens to find himself on the rough shoulder of the road just inches from going off into a deep ravine, that person is likely to experience fear. And the fear will be the genuine wake-up call to the person: *Pull off and get some rest, or you'll be in big trouble!*

Emotions mobilize us into action.

Fear tends to mobilize us to protect ourselves. (This is not a spiritual fear, but the normal emotion of fear, such as fear of falling, fear of danger, and so forth.) This fear compels us not to touch a hot stove.

Anger mobilizes us to seek ways in which to correct wrongs—both those done against us and those done against loved ones.

Love compels us to relate to one another and to God, to fulfill the needs of others, and to fulfill our need for satisfaction and meaning in life.

Desire mobilizes us to obtain or possess, to get the things we need for our psychological, emotional, and spiritual well-being. Desire is at the root of all ambition to seek rewards of all kinds.

I feel certain that you can identify ways in which these four emotions have compelled you or people you know to certain types of behavior. Identify some of the behaviors, both good and bad.

Emotion	Behavior That Resulted
Fear	Good:
	Bad:
Anger	Good:
	Bad:
Love	Good:
	Bad:
Desire	Good:
	Bad:

A Purpose of Pleasure

When we manifest emotions in good behavior, beauty, harmony, mutual benefit, and growth result. When we manifest emotions in bad behavior, we find discord, estrangement, destruction, and sin.

Furthermore, when we manifest emotions in right ways, we

experience lasting enjoyment—the fun itself may be temporary, but it is a pleasure to recall. When we manifest emotions in wrong ways, we may experience temporary enjoyment, but the pleasure is fleeting and the memory of the occasion is painful. The expression of emotion always has about it an element of pleasure or enjoyment. I have no doubt that this is a second reason that God gave us emotions: so that we might experience pleasure, fun, good times, warm relationships, and satisfying feelings.

God intends for His people to enjoy life. The fruit of the Holy Spirit is expressed as *joy!* We are to delight in God's creation, in friendships, in marriage, in parenting. We are to enjoy the work and ministry opportunities that God puts before us. God has given us the emotional equipment necessary for experiencing pleasure, self-fulfillment, and self-satisfaction.

When we deny ourselves all opportunities truly to enjoy life—with gusto, with enthusiasm, with energy—we miss out on the fullness of life God desires for us. For too many people, pleasure has become equated with sin; enjoyment has become equated with irreverence.

That isn't the way God designed life. He wants us to experience pleasure and to know how to have a good time without sinning. He wants us to be passionate people, especially in godly expressions of love and caring for others. He wants us to enjoy all that He gives us, does for us, and imparts to us, and to respond with exuberant, energetic, joyful praise, thanksgiving, and acts of worship.

The Christian life was never intended to be stripped of emotions. Rather, Christians are to manifest a full, abundant, overflowing range of emotions in behavior that honors God and shows respect for others.

- *What new insights do you have about God's creation of emotions and the purpose of emotions in your life?*

How Do Our Emotions Relate to Behavior?

Our emotions work in a very basic way, common to both men and women. Emotions are attached to every thought. We have a way of "feeling" about every idea we entertain.

We allow a thought or idea to take root in our minds, we visualize that thought taking place in reality, and then we make a decision in the will about how to respond. The degree to which our emotions are a part of this process—in giving birth to the idea, in enhancing the visualization, and in compelling us to make a decision—determines how quickly and how intensely we will act on the idea.

The Scriptures tell us about humankind, "As he thinks in his heart, so is he" (Prov. 23:7). What you choose to think about—or allow yourself to think about—gets you into trouble far more than your emotions. It is your thought life that you are to govern with diligence. Avoid activities that you know are going to feed negative or sinful thoughts and images into your mind.

You must go out of your way to halt the flood of violent, seductive, and tempting messages that come to you unsolicited and undesired. Turn off the dial, turn away your eyes, turn down certain invitations, and in many cases, you'll be sparing yourself the agony of dealing with an overwhelming number of ungodly ideas. Once sinful images and ideas have entered your mind, your emotions will be engaged regarding them. Your willpower will be required to make a decision about how to respond. It is much easier to avert or deny the input of negative, potentially harmful ideas than to exert willpower needed to keep from responding to them, often to your detriment spiritually.

- *Can you recall a time when you found it very difficult not to act on an idea or image that had rooted itself into your mind and engaged your emotional response to it?*

_____

_____

The Foundation for Controlling Emotions

Repeatedly in this study guide, you will find the word *control* linked to emotions. What exactly does control mean?

First, let's deal with four other alternatives people take in responding to their emotions:

1. Repression. When people repress their emotions, they refuse to admit that they have feelings. They may deny the existence of one or more very specific emotions. For example, they may refuse to admit that they feel angry or discouraged or depressed. Some people attempt to repress all emotions, however, for various reasons we'll discuss in the next lesson. Repression is unhealthy for the person, and it can lead to behaviors that cause harm to others.

2. Stifling. When people have emotional responses but refuse to give them expression, they are stifling their emotions. They may have an "I can't" or an "I won't" orientation. They feel a deep agitation inside, but for either "can't" or "won't" reasons, they refuse to give expression to what they feel. The result is often immense frustration. Some people refer to this as stuffing emotions inside.

If people continue to stifle what they feel, they may find the emotions building to an eruption point later in life, or they may find their pent-up emotions eating away at them, resulting in physical or psychological illness.

3. Drifting. Some people never pay attention to their emotions. They simply drift along in them, figuring that emotions come and go.

If we experience emotions and don't face up to them and deal with them, they can become entrenched in us. They can become more firmly rooted in us rather than dissipate or disappear.

For example, if a person is angry in one situation, but that anger is allowed to run its course without intervention, resolution, or some sense of control by the will, that anger can become the foundation for a pattern in the person's life. The next time the person is angry, the new anger builds on the previous anger. The behavior associated with the anger may be more volatile or violent. Over time, the person may become an angry person—ready to be ignited at any time. When emotions drift without control they become deeply ingrained in the personality.

4. Praying for deliverance. I have met a number of people who choose to pray for deliverance from certain emotions rather than face up to the fact that they need to control their emotions. They want God to take away their capacity for anger, loneliness, fear, discouragement, and so forth rather than learn to deal with these emotions and grow in an ability to use them constructively in their lives.

A prayer I hear often is, "Lord, deliver me from impatience." That sounds like a good prayer on the surface, but let's consider what would happen if the Lord really did deliver you from impatience. You would lose your frustration at not having things done on your timetable and in your way, and you would probably lose any desire to pursue good goals. Your ambition would be squelched. You would allow many things to slide by unchallenged and uncorrected. You may easily become nonchalant in your attitude and lackadaisical toward sin.

Do you really want to be without ambition? Do you really want to lose your drive in life and not achieve your full potential? Do you really want to become so patient with evil and sin that you do nothing to defeat the enemy of your soul? I doubt that's what you want!

Rather than pray for deliverance from emotions, you need to pray for God to give you wisdom in how to deal with your emotions and how to control them in ways that are in keeping with His Word and His plan for your life.

- *Have you tended to repress, stifle, drift, or seek deliverance for emotions as alternatives to learning how to control your emotions?*

_____

_____

- *In what ways do you feel challenged by the Lord to pursue greater emotional health today?*

The Process of Controlling Emotions

How then can you truly control your emotions?

1. Experience the new birth in Christ Jesus. You can't control your emotions by yourself. You need the help of the Holy Spirit, and the Holy Spirit's help is made available only to those who accept the sacrifice that Jesus Christ made on the cross, receive God's forgiveness, and open their lives to the indwelling presence and power of the Holy Spirit.

If you truly want to control your emotions today, ask Jesus to become the Lord of your life and to fill you with His Holy Spirit.

If you are already a Christian, ask the Holy Spirit to help you to control your emotions and to change the emotional responses you have that may be damaging or in error.

2. Examine your dominant thoughts. What do you think about most often? What you think about today is what you become tomorrow. As you examine your thoughts, be aware of the feelings associated with them. If your dominant thought is about how a person has wronged you and what you might do in response, consider your feelings. Are you angry, disappointed, frustrated, or perplexed? Your feelings are going to have a great impact on the course of action you begin to imagine and eventually may choose to take.

3. Exchange thoughts and feelings that are contrary to God's Word. When you truly take inventory of your thoughts and the feelings associated with them, you may find that what you are thinking and feeling is *not* what would be pleasing to God. To know fully what is pleasing to God, of course, you need to have an understanding of what the Bible says.

Once you have identified a thought pattern—or a set of emotional responses to a thought or idea—that is not in line with God's Word, ask the Lord to help you change the way you are thinking and feeling. Choose to have a different set of responses. Choose to think about something else. Choose to feel in a different way. A change of this type often takes patience, love (of yourself and a growing love of others), and a genuine desire to pursue a godly life.

Identify what you would rather be thinking about. Identify the way you would like to feel. Be aware that in choosing to think about something other than what has occupied your mind, you must choose something pleasing to God. In identifying a new emotional response, you must choose something that is in keeping with God's plan and desire for you. Exchanging one harmful thought and emotion for another certainly is not what the Lord wants.

4. Exercise your powerful privilege of prayer. Thank the Lord in prayer for changing your thoughts and feelings to conform with His Word and the life manifested by the Lord Jesus Christ. State your prayer in positive terms: "Thank You, Lord, that You will teach me to trust, You will help me to overcome, You will give me this new feeling as my automatic response toward this situation or person." Such a prayer can result in strengthening your faith and renewing your mind.

5. Expect God's healing to begin immediately. You may not feel the Lord healing you of harmful thoughts and emotions immediately, but you can start believing for God's healing immediately. Believing is the forerunner of all spiritual realities. In turn, spiritual realities are the forerunner of all physical and material realities. You may not see the fullness of God's healing at work in your life for some time, but you can expect and believe that God's healing has begun in you.

Why pray for healing of thought patterns and emotional responses? Because ultimately, the damaging emotional responses that are not controlled or that are not changed can bring about great harm in your life. They can result in physical ailments too numerous to recount, as well as psychological or mental illness. They can result in flawed, unhealthy, or shattered relationships.

A failure to control your emotions—which may include correcting or changing your emotional responses to life—can be devastating, especially if your errant emotions lead you to sin or cause others to sin. The end result of sin is death, both literally and figuratively.

* *Have you had an experience in which the Lord led you to change your dominant thoughts and your emotional responses?*

_____

_____

God's Desire for You: Strong, Healthy Emotions

The Lord desires that you have strong, healthy emotions subjected to the control of the Holy Spirit at work in your life. The Lord created emotions for your good, and He desires that you draw benefit and pleasure from being a person who can have a "feeling" response to Him and to others.

Make it your prayer today that you will ask the Lord to help you develop healthy emotions. Ask Him to give you the courage to exhibit or manifest your emotions in appropriate and healthy ways to the benefit of yourself and others.

* *What new insights do you have into emotions?*

_____

_____

* *In what ways do you feel challenged today?*

_____

_____

LESSON 3

A HEALTHY EMOTIONAL RESPONSE TO LIFE

- Emotions are good.
- Emotions are our friends.
- Emotions are a sign of strength.
- Emotions are to be encouraged.

How many times do you hear statements such as these? Probably not often. In most cases when emotions are discussed, they are couched in disparaging terms. They are regarded as something to be avoided or squelched.

In this lesson we're going to look at some of the false notions about emotions and what God's Word says about emotional health.

Clearing Up the Errors About Emotions

People seem to have five erroneous ideas about emotions:

1. "I'm just not an emotional person." Men usually make this statement. The person really means, "I don't express my emotions freely, properly, or in a healthy way." The person is missing out on a great deal of enjoyment in life. The fact is, every person is an *emotional* person. Each person is born with a capacity for having emotions and expressing them. Babies cry; they smile; they respond to pleasure and pain; they become angry, show fear, and cuddle in response to love.

Proper Expression

Proper expression of emotions refers to the match between an emotion and a behavior. It's proper to show grief by crying. It may also be proper to show anger or happiness by crying. Conversely, it is not proper to show grief by laughing. Some people have never learned the proper way to express their emotional response to life's events, and because they are unsure of themselves, they deny themselves any expression of emotions.

Appropriate Expression

Appropriate expression of emotions refers to the context in which an emotion is expressed. At some times and places it may be inappropriate to express certain emotions. For example, dissolving into a puddle of tears before your boss or your employees may seem inappropriate to you. Your decision not to express emotion at certain times or places, or in the presence of certain people, is not a denial of emotions, but an example of controlling your emotions until you can express them fully in an appropriate setting or in the presence of people with whom you feel comfortable.

Jesus was an emotional person. The Bible offers numerous examples of His expressing emotions. The actions of Jesus in the gospel accounts show that He felt sorrow and grief, loneliness (or aloneness), frustration and anger, love and concern (compassion), and many more feelings along the full spectrum of emotions. Jesus knows what we feel because He has felt what we feel.

Consider the verses below in the light of proper response and appropriate behavior.

What the Word Says	What the Word Says to Me
When Jesus saw her weeping, and the Jews who came with her weeping, He groaned in the spirit and was troubled. And He said, "Where have you laid him?" They said to Him, "Lord, come and see." Jesus wept. Then the Jews said, "See how He loved him!" (John 11:33–36).	_____
He was withdrawn from them about a stone's throw, and He knelt down and prayed, saying, "Father, if it is Your will, take this cup away from Me; nevertheless not My will, but Yours, be done." Then an angel appeared to Him from heaven, strengthening Him. And being in agony, He prayed more earnestly. Then His sweat became like great drops of blood falling down to the ground (Luke 22:41–44).	_____

2. *"Expressing emotions is a sign of weakness."* The person who says this is usually uncomfortable with weakness.

We are all weak at times. Even people who may appear generally weak to us sometimes are very strong in certain situations. In my opinion, it is a strong person who expresses emotions—and also a healthy person. It is a weak person who represses emotions. A person with extremely low self-esteem often has difficulty expressing emotions.

It is not weak to cry in the privacy of your own room after a loved one has died, betrayed you, or abandoned you. It is not weak to admit to others that you have been angry, disappointed, frustrated, or lonely on occasion. It is not weak to tell your child that you love her and to do so with a hug.

The Scriptures tell us that Jesus "rejoiced in the Spirit" (Luke 10:21) when He heard the good report from the seventy disciples He had sent out to preach the gospel. Jesus was willing to show others that He was happy! I know people who don't show others they are pleased or happy about something out of fear that someone may take advantage of them. Jesus never had that attitude. His rejoicing was not weakness; it was a spontaneous emotional response to good news.

3. *"Emotions are enemies."* People who say this usually have been betrayed by their emotions at times when they failed to control their emotions or when they expressed their emotions inappropriately. Our emotions are assets when they are controlled.

- *Have you had experiences in which you were manipulated by the emotions of others?*

_____

_____

equated emotions with weakness?

_____

_____

failed to control your emotions and experienced detriment or a loss as a result?

_____

_____

- *In each instance, how did you feel as a result?*

_____

_____

4. *"Emotions are unrelated to the human spirit."* Perhaps nothing could be farther from the truth. Our emotions are closely linked with our spiritual development. We have both opinions about God and feelings toward God, and the feelings we have toward God are often much more basic and long-standing in our lives than our opinions. In fact, our opinions about God are often based on our feelings!

I tend to hear this statement when people have sought out a counselor to help them deal with a problem in their lives, often a problem involving deep-seated feelings. They think it is acceptable to seek out any trained professional counselor to help them with their emotional problems, regardless of the counselor's faith in Jesus Christ or the counselor's desire to help others from a Christian perspective.

If you are seeking counseling for any problem in your life, find a Christian counselor. Every area of your life is linked to your spirit and to your faith, especially the areas with a strong emotional component. The more feelings associated with a problem, or the greater your depth of feeling about an issue, person, or problem, the greater your need for a *Christian* counselor.

5. *"The best approach to emotions is to let them all out."* This approach may make the person feel better, but this is not the wisdom of God. We do not live unto ourselves. We are responsible for the way we behave toward others and in the presence of others.

Again, we come back to appropriateness. Sometimes certain emotions should *not* be expressed in the presence of certain people or under certain conditions. Learning when to let your emotions out, and when to hold them in until you are by yourself or in a different setting, is a vital part of learning how to control your emotions. The person who lets them all out is egocentric and uncaring.

- *Have you had any experiences with people who let all their emotions out to their detriment or to the detriment of a relationship or another person?*

_____

_____

God's Picture of Emotional Health

Jesus is our role model in expressing emotions appropriately. He had perfect emotional health.

Jesus clearly displayed four basic tenets of emotional health:

1. Rely on God. Jesus placed His trust squarely in the Father. He didn't rely on the religious structure of the day, the world's systems, or anything else to help Him accomplish His purpose in life. He relied on His heavenly Father for everything He needed.

Rely on the Lord for your health, protection, daily provision, purpose in life, ability and capability, strength, courage, and wisdom. With Him, all things are possible.

To feel emotionally secure and healthy, you must place your total trust in God and believe that He will take care of you, protect you, and love you regardless of what anyone else says or does to you.

The emotionally healthy person may be alone and experience temporary loneliness, but ultimately, such a person knows that God is present always and that there is no greater Friend than Jesus.

What the Word Says	What the Word Says to Me
I can do all things through Christ who strengthens me (Phil. 4:13).	_____ _____ _____
There is a friend who sticks closer than a brother (Prov. 18:24).	_____ _____ _____
[Jesus said,] "Most assuredly, I say to you, the Son can do nothing of Himself, but what He sees the Father do; for whatever He does, the Son also does in like manner" (John 5:19).	_____ _____ _____ _____ _____

• *In what ways do you feel challenged to trust God more, especially regarding your emotional responses to life?*

_____

_____

2. Give generously to others. Jesus never withheld a miracle from anyone who asked Him for one. He freely preached the good news to all who were willing to hear. He was willing to risk pain and harm, even rejection and death, to make Himself available to all.

The person with healthy emotions is willing to risk love. The emotionally healthy person openly expresses care, concern, and compassion.

The emotion of love is always manifested in some form of giving. The emotionally healthy person loves generously and, therefore, gives generously in as many ways as possible, to as many people as possible, as often as possible.

What the Word Says

[Jesus said,] "Judge not, and you shall not be judged. Condemn not, and you shall not be con-demned. Forgive, and you will be forgiven. Give, and it will be given to you: good measure, pressed down, shaken together, and running over will be put into your bosom. For with the same measure that you use, it will be measured back to you" (Luke 6:37–38).

If someone says, "I love God," and hates his brother, he is a liar; for he who does not love his

What the Word Says to Me

_____

_____

_____

_____

_____

_____

_____

_____

_____

_____

_____

_____

_____

_____

_____

brother whom he has seen, how	_____
can he love God whom he has	_____
not seen? And this command-	_____
ment we have from Him: that he	_____
who loves God must love his	_____
brother also (1 John 4:20–21).	_____

- *In what ways do you feel challenged to give more freely of yourself to others?*

_____

_____

3. *Continually ask for the Holy Spirit's guidance.* Everything that Jesus did was revealed to Him by the Father. Today, we must ask the Holy Spirit to reveal the Father's will to us.

The emotionally healthy person may feel anger, for example, but in asking the Holy Spirit for guidance in how to channel that anger into positive behavior, the person is going to find an outlet for anger that results in blessing, not harm. The emotionally healthy person may feel disappointment or discouragement, but in asking the Holy Spirit for guidance in what to do to relieve the feelings, the person is going to be led to new opportunities or new relationships that will result in hope.

Continual reliance on the Holy Spirit takes the form of continual prayer. To pray is to talk to God, and you are wise to talk to God around the clock, every day of the week. (See 1 Thess. 5:17.)

What the Word Says	**What the Word Says to Me**
Trust in the LORD with all your heart,	_____
	_____
And lean not on your own under- standing;	_____
	_____
In all your ways acknowledge	_____

Him,
And He shall direct your paths
(Prov. 3:5–6).

[Jesus said,] "I am the vine, you
are the branches. He who abides
in Me, and I in him, bears much
fruit; for without Me you can do
nothing" (John 15:5).

- *In what ways do you feel challenged to rely on guidance from the Holy Spirit, especially regarding your emotional response to situations that arise daily?*

_____

_____

4. Recognize the true spiritual enemy. Jesus had numerous confrontations with people who denied His divinity, questioned His authority, and attempted to undermine His teachings and miracles. But Jesus always recognized that His true enemy was Satan.

We have countless experiences in which we feel negative emotions—hurt, anger, frustration, disappointment, worry, discouragement. Our first response is usually to try to even the score with the person who has hurt us. Ultimately, our battle is not with the person, but with the true enemy of our souls, the devil.

The emotionally healthy person does not seek revenge or retaliation against others, but resorts to prayer, to giving, and to blessing.

What the Word Says

[Jesus said,] "The thief does not
come except to steal, and to kill,
and to destroy. I have come that

What the Word Says to me

they may have life, and that they
may have it more abundantly"
(John 10:10).

_____

_____

_____

Put on the whole armor of God,
that you may be able to stand
against the wiles of the devil
(Eph. 6:11).

_____

_____

_____

_____

- *In what ways do you feel challenged to confront the one who desires to keep you in bondage to damaging emotions?*

_____

_____

A Desire for Wholeness

Are you willing to turn away from all repressing, drifting, or seeking deliverance from emotions, and seek instead to control your emotions? Do you desire to base your emotional health on the same principles reflected in the life of Jesus Christ?

The first step toward emotional wholeness is to make a decision with your will that you desire to pursue emotional health and strength, and that you desire for your emotional life to be in harmony with your spiritual life—a whole life founded on Christ Jesus.

- *What new insights do you have regarding your emotions?*

_____

_____

THE FOUNDATION FOR HEALTHY EMOTIONS

Do you like the person you see in the mirror in the morning? Liking yourself relates to self-image, which is not limited to your physical appearance. Self-image includes the total you—personality, talents and abilities, accomplishments, desires and goals, and spiritual relationship with the Lord. Your emotional health is rooted strongly in your self-image, as are your relationships with family members and friends. Nearly all of your behavior is based on who you think you are and how you feel about yourself.

The apostle Paul wrote an interesting statement to the Christians in Corinth:

> For I am the least of the apostles, who am not worthy to be called an apostle, because I persecuted the church of God. But by the grace of God I am what I am, and His grace toward me was not in vain; but I labored more abundantly than they all, yet not I, but the grace of God which was with me (1 Cor. 15:9–10).

On the surface, Paul appeared to be putting himself down. He appeared to be saying, "I am nothing. I am worthless." A closer reading of this statement, however, taken in context, reveals the exact opposite. Paul had a very healthy self-image!

This passage is part of an argument Paul was making to the Corinthians, who were arguing about whether they should heed Paul's words to them or listen to other prophets who came into their midst. At the beginning of chapter 15, Paul reminded them that the gospel he had preached to them resulted in their salvation: Jesus Christ died for our sins, was buried, and rose the third day as was witnessed by Peter, the apostles, more than five hundred followers of Jesus, and Paul himself.

In saying that he was "least" of all the apostles, Paul was stating that he was the last among those he named to have witnessed the resurrected Christ, and that of all those named, he spent the least amount of time with Jesus. But, Paul said, "by the grace of God I am what I am"—which was an apostle, a born-again believer in Christ Jesus, an ardent follower of Jesus. Paul had spent a limited amount of time with the Corinthians, but that wasn't what counted. What he did with the time mattered in God's eyes.

Paul also said that God's grace toward him was not in vain—that he received Christ into his life, he labored hard to witness of Christ to others, and God's grace has continued to work through his life as others accepted the Lord.

This powerful and positive statement from Paul reveals his strength of character and his strong self-image. Paul was not putting himself down. He was simply stating facts about his life, the foremost one of which—in his opinion—was that everything he was and did was in keeping with God's saving grace.

Ultimately, your self-image is linked to who you are in Christ Jesus. If you have no relationship with Christ, it will be very difficult for you to have a strong, healthy self-image. If you have a relationship with Christ, however, you have accepted—to at least some degree—the fact that God so loved you that He sent Jesus to die for your sins so that you could have eternal life. (See John 3:16.)

Do you know with certainty today that

- God loves you infinitely, unconditionally, and eternally?

- God stands ready to forgive you of all your sins and trespasses against Him and others?
- Jesus Christ valued your life so much that He gave His life so that you might live forever with Him and the Father in heaven?
- you are being transformed more and more into the likeness of Jesus Christ as the Holy Spirit works in and through your life?

If you can say yes to these questions, you have a firm basis for a heathy self-image.

Unfortunately, even people who believe that Jesus died for their sins, that God loves them, that they stand forgiven before God, and that they are being transformed into the perfection and wholeness of Jesus Christ sometimes have difficulty loving themselves. Friend, if God loves you and has forgiven you, you should love yourself. If God says you are that valuable, you are! If the Holy Spirit of almighty God is continually at work bringing you to a place of refinement and perfection, surely you are a beloved, highly cherished child of God!

However, nobody can force you to see the truth of God's love and redemption in your life or make you accept the fact that you are infinitely valuable to God. You must paint on your mental and emotional canvas the image that reflects what you believe to be true about yourself.

What the Word Says	What the Word Says to Me
In this is love, not that we loved God, but that He loved us and sent His Son to be the propitiation for our sins. Beloved, if God so loved us, we also ought to love one another (1 John 4:10–11).	_____ _____ _____ _____ _____ _____
We also, since the day we heard	_____

it, do not cease to pray for you, and to ask that you may be filled with the knowledge of His will in all wisdom and spiritual understanding; that you may walk worthy of the Lord, fully pleasing Him, being fruitful in every good work and increasing in the knowledge of God; strengthened with all might, according to His glorious power, for all patience and longsuffering with joy; giving thanks to the Father who has qualified us to be partakers of the inheritance of the saints in the light. He has delivered us from the power of darkness and conveyed us into the kingdom of the Son of His love, in whom we have redemption through His blood, the forgiveness of sins (Col. 1:9–14).

As Christians, our worth and self-image *must* flow from Christ Jesus. We are worthy because He declares us to be worthy.

The Importance of a Parent's Words

Children draw much of their self-image from their parents. To a great extent, the ability of the parent to impart good self-worth and a positive self-image is based on the parent's self-image and the parent's understanding of God's work in the child's life. If you have a poor self-image today, you must recognize that you have been taught that self-image. Your parents and others who had influence over you in your early childhood likely instilled it in you.

It is counterproductive, however, to blame your parents, teachers, and others in your childhood for what you are and do today. In most cases, they didn't intend to impart to you a negative self-image. As an adult, you can make new choices. You can choose to believe the truth about what God says in His Word, and especially what God says about you as His beloved child.

Forgive your parents for their failure to instill in you a good self-image, and move forward in your life. Accept what your heavenly Father has to say to you and about you.

Even if every parent was a master at instilling a positive self-image in the children, each child eventually faces the fact of the personal sin nature, which can be a major blow to self-image.

Adam and Eve were created perfect—complete and whole—as human beings. Then they sinned. As a result of their sin, they tried to hide from God and from each other. In hiding from God and each other, they began to hide from themselves—they tried to justify their behavior to God. (Self-justification always involves some degree of attempting to hide from the truth.) Adam and Eve found it extremely difficult to accept that they were no longer perfect.

Even people with healthy self-esteem must face this same reality. No one is perfect. No one is whole or complete. All of us are in need of a Savior and of the presence of the Holy Spirit in our lives to transform us into the likeness of Christ Jesus.

Just as we must not blame our parents for our lack of a positive self-image as adults, so we must not attempt to blame anyone else for the sinful nature we inherited as our birthright. We must accept full responsibility for our self-image.

- *In what ways do you feel challenged today about your self-image?*

_____

_____

Hallmarks of a Positive Self-Image

The person with a good self-image

- is able to accept both the good and the bad in himself.
- is open to a relationship with God and with others.
- expresses love freely and willingly, but always within the constraints of God's will.
- is willing to expose his innermost feelings and ideas.
- is confident of *God's* ability at work in and through his life (acknowledging that God is the source of all his ability and the One who reinforces and undergirds every effort).
- accommodates failures, learns from them, and moves forward.

The person with a positive self-image sees that God—and future growth and development made possible by God—can more than make up for anything missing.

What the Word Says	What the Word Says to Me
Whatever things are true, whatever things are noble, whatever things are just, whatever things are pure, whatever things are lovely, whatever things are of good report, if there is any virtue and if there is anything praiseworthy—meditate on these things (Phil. 4:8).	
Become complete. Be of good comfort, be of one mind, live in peace; and the God of love and	

peace will be with you (2 Cor.
13:11).

Things That Destroy a Good Self-Image

Your self-image gives you a sense of worth, a sense that you are valuable to the kingdom of God. When you have a good self-image, you are more willing to make yourself available to do God's work. Therefore, it is vital not only for your sake, but also for the sake of the gospel, that you acquire and maintain a good self-image rooted in Christ Jesus.

At least five things can result when your self-image takes a "hit." Be aware of them. Avoid them. They are traps to keep you from being fully effective in serving the Lord.

1. The trap of guilt. Even after you have received God's forgiveness of your sin nature and have accepted Jesus Christ as your Savior and Lord, you have the potential to commit sin. Indeed, you do sin. And with sin comes guilt.

Unless you go to the Lord each time you are aware that you have sinned and ask for His forgiveness and help in not sinning further, you are likely to develop a growing mountain of guilt.

The more guilt you feel, the more you begin to question, How can God bless me? How can God use me now? Self-image begins to disintegrate, and if you continue to amass guilt and not seek forgiveness, you can become so overwhelmed by guilt that you become immobilized and ineffective in your Christian witness.

Continually ask God's forgiveness for your sins. Don't accumulate guilt.

What the Word Says

If we confess our sins, He is faithful and just to forgive us our sins and to cleanse us from all unrighteousness (1 John 1:9).

What the Word Says to Me

_____

_____

_____

_____

If you confess with your mouth
the Lord Jesus and believe in
your heart that God has raised
Him from the dead, you will be
saved. For with the heart one believes unto righteousness, and
with the mouth confession is
made unto salvation (Rom. 10:9–
10).

2. The trap of overachievement. If you attempt to do it all—either because you are driven to achieve or because you don't trust others to help in a task—you run a risk of exhaustion. When you collapse in exhaustion and face the fact that you haven't been able to do everything you thought you could or would do, you are likely to become discouraged. Self-image takes a blow when you experience discouragement.

The best way to stay out of the trap of overachievement is to ask the Lord every day what He desires for you to do during the day. Then if you can't do all that, ask the Lord to help you readjust your priorities or manage your time better, or ask Him to enlarge your ability. Live one day at a time.

Learn to break down large tasks into smaller tasks, to set achievable goals for yourself at each stage of a large project, and to set aside time in your schedule for prayer, Bible reading, physical exercise, and relaxation. Get sufficient sleep. And above all, let the peace of God rule your life. The Lord will not ask you to do more than you can do and still keep your life in balance.

What the Word Says

What the Word Says to Me

For by grace you have been saved
through faith, and that not of
yourselves; it is the gift of God,

not of works, lest anyone should
boast. For we are His workman-
ship, created in Christ Jesus for
good works, which God prepared
beforehand that we should walk
in them (Eph. 2:8-10).

The righteous and the wise and
their works are in the hand of
God (Eccl. 9:1).

3. The trap of criticism. People who are willing to listen to every
bit of criticism leveled against them, and who generally take it to
heart, have a great need for others to approve of them.

In the final analysis, the only approval you need is that of the
Lord Jesus. His approval is based on your desire to follow Him
and to live according to His commandments. It is not based on
your achievements, accomplishments, possessions, status, or level
of income. If you diligently seek to love and serve the Lord, you
have God's approval!

Don't listen to people who continually try to knock you down.
Don't listen to people who criticize you no matter what you do.
Such criticism is like a hammer against your self-image. Although
it may be wise for you to take good counsel in improving certain
skills or abilities, it is unwise for you to listen to those who
continually seek to make you a better person according to *their*
standards. The only standards you need to be concerned about are
ones in God's Word.

What the Word Says

What the Word Says to Me

Therefore let us pursue the
things which make for peace and
the things by which one may ed-
ify another (Rom. 14:19).

We are bound to thank God always for you, brethren, as it is fit-
ting, because your faith grows
exceedingly, and the love of
every one of you all abounds toward each other (2 Thess. 1:3).

_____

_____

_____

_____

_____

_____

4. The trap of comparison. This trap is very close in nature to the trap of criticism. Some people continually gauge their performance by comparing themselves to others. They are much more concerned with being, having, owning, or achieving *the* best than in giving their best effort.

Not everybody can be number one all the time. If you continually try to best all those around you, you are likely to suffer a major blow to your self-image each time you come in second best. The greater the failure, the greater the blow to the self-image.

Jesus Christ is established as our role model in the Scriptures. We are to grow up spiritually to become like Him. That does not mean, however, that we will ever *be* Christ. He is the only perfect Man who ever lived, 100 percent divine while being 100 percent human. We are not going to experience His perfection. Even so, the Holy Spirit is at work in us to transform us more and more into His likeness.

If you are a Christian yielded to the Holy Spirit's work within you, you are not the same person today that you were last year. And you won't be the same person this time next year that you are today. You are *growing* toward wholeness.

Every time you are tempted to compare your accomplishments with those of someone else, concentrate on doing your best.

What the Word Says

What the Word Says to Me

You are no longer strangers and
foreigners, but fellow citizens
with the saints and members of
the household of God, having

_____

_____

_____

_____

been built on the foundation of   _____
the apostles and prophets, Jesus   _____
Christ Himself being the chief   _____
cornerstone, in whom the whole   _____
building, being fitted together,   _____
grows into a holy temple in the   _____
Lord, in whom you also are be-   _____
ing built together for a dwelling   _____
place of God in the Spirit (Eph.   _____
2:19–22).   _____

Aspire to lead a quiet life, to   _____
mind your own business, and to   _____
work with your own hands, as we   _____
commanded you (1 Thess. 4:11).   _____

5. The trap of scriptural error. Some people fall into the trap of error because they read the Scriptures incorrectly or they have been taught the Scriptures incorrectly. Let me give you two examples.

Luke 14:11 says, "Whoever exalts himself will be humbled, and he who humbles himself will be exalted." Some people have been taught that this means we should never receive a compliment or take credit for what we have done. To the contrary! Jesus made the statement in a very specific setting. He told a parable to some people who were invited to a party and were vying for the best seats at the dinner table. He taught that the better approach was to take a lesser position of honor. That way, if the host invited you to a more honorable position, you would be given increased respect among those present. But if you took the best seat and then the host asked you to take a lesser one, you would be subject to scorn and embarrassment. In that context, the one who exalts himself is in a position to be humbled; the one who humbles himself is in a position to be exalted.

This passage has nothing to do with self-image or self-esteem.

Throughout the Bible, we are admonished to treat other people with kindness, respect, and honor. We are to serve others, give to others, and let others have their say and make their choices. But at no time are we told to deny the value that the Lord places upon us as His beloved children. There is a difference between being a kindhearted person and a person who has no regard for her talents, abilities, or stature in Christ.

Philippians 2:3 is often taught in error. It says, "Let nothing be done through selfish ambition or conceit, but in lowliness of mind let each esteem others better than himself." Some people have been taught that this means you should always give way to other people, saints and sinners alike. Paul was speaking directly to the body of Christ. He was calling on the church at Philippi to be "like-minded, having the same love, being of one accord, of one mind" in Christ Jesus (Phil. 2:2). He wanted God's people to get along in peace and harmony in the pursuit of God's will for them all. To that end, he told them not to pursue their self-interests or to think of themselves individually as better than the whole church. Rather, they should consider what was of benefit to the entire body of Christ. Paul continued by teaching, "Let each of you look out not only for his own interests, but also for the interests of others" (Phil. 2:4).

There is great balance in what Paul teaches. On the one hand, he calls upon the church to be bold in dealing with sin, evil, and the assaults of the devil. On the other hand, he calls upon the church members to be loving and generous with one another. We are to be alive in Christ, even as we are "dead" to all carnal influences that seek to destroy us. Paul carried this message to every church where he ministered.

You can be bold in denouncing evil and loving your brothers and sisters in Christ without any form of self-deprecation or self-hate.

What the Word Says	What the Word Says to Me
Fear the LORD, serve Him in sincerity and in truth (Josh. 24:14).	_____ _____

Be diligent to present yourself approved to God, a worker who does not need to be ashamed, rightly dividing the word of truth (2 Tim. 2:15).

_____
_____
_____
_____
_____

All Scripture is given by inspiration of God, and is profitable for doctrine, for reproof, for correction, for instruction in righteousness, that the man of God may be complete, thoroughly equipped for every good work (2 Tim. 3:16–17).

_____
_____
_____
_____
_____
_____
_____
_____

- *What new insights do you have about the foundation of your self-esteem and how it affects your emotional health and wellbeing?*

  _____

  _____

- *In what ways are you being challenged by the Lord in the area of your emotions?*

  _____

  _____

SEVEN KEYS TO EMOTIONAL WHOLENESS

It is not enough merely to know the foundation for sound emotions or to understand the relationship between a positive self-image and emotional well-being. You must take the steps necessary to move from emotional weakness to emotional strength. The ideas in this lesson are related to all of the following lessons, so I encourage you to refer to this lesson often.

There are at least seven major aspects of wholeness involved in seeking God's best for your emotional life. You do not need to take them in sequence. Rather, they are like having a ring of keys—all of which need to be inserted and turned simultaneously. These keys are habits that you must build into your life in an ongoing manner. As you do so, I have no doubt that you will become more and more whole in your spirit, including your emotions.

Key #1: Give Your Heart to Christ

Spiritual redemption is the first key toward developing a positive self-image. People who don't know Christ may claim that they think the world of themselves, but they won't draw that conclusion if they are honest. Most unbelievers I know who state that they are self-sufficient in themselves and don't need Christ are miserable people in crises. They are like beautiful flowering weeds with no strong root system.

They have only themselves upon which to rely for strength, energy, enthusiasm, creativity, and new methods. Eventually, they get to the end of themselves. They do not have the Holy Spirit resident in them to build them up in Christ in a way that is based on truth and is comforting even in times of chastisement.

Having a relationship with Christ Jesus resolves many issues that undermine emotional wholeness:

- *Feeling guilty.* Guilt is created when you have unforgiven sin. When you ask for God's forgiveness, you are forgiven. Guilt is washed away.
- *Feeling unloved.* When you turn to Christ, you must accept, at least at some level, that God loves you and desires to have an eternal relationship with you.
- *Having a spirit of revenge against others.* Once you have accepted God's free gift of salvation to you—acknowledging your sin and need of a Savior—you are no longer in a position to attempt to justify why God should not forgive others who are also sinners and in need of a Savior. What God has done for you, He desires to do for all men and women, regardless of their past.
- *Striving to earn favor with God.* God's gift of salvation to you is free. You can't earn it, buy it, or achieve it through good works. You don't deserve it. When you truly are born anew spiritually, you must accept that any favor you have with God is on the basis of what *Christ* has done, is doing, and will do in you and through you.

If you truly want to be emotionally whole today, give your life to Christ.

Once you have accepted Christ Jesus as your personal Savior, you must follow Him as your Lord. This daily following of Christ calls you to a frequent request for God's forgiveness—a daily cleansing of your spirit that is just as vital to your spiritual health as a daily bath is to your physical health. You seek God's forgiveness first for your sin nature and then for the sins you commit in your human, error-prone nature as you follow Christ.

No one is capable of following Christ perfectly. Everyone is prone to both willful and innocent errors—what some call sins of commission and sins of omission. It is for these sins that you seek ongoing forgiveness.

What the Word Says	What the Word Says to Me
The LORD your God is gracious and merciful, and will not turn His face from you if you return to Him (2 Chron. 30:9).	_____ _____ _____ _____
[Jesus said,] "The one who comes to Me I will by no means cast out" (John 6:37).	_____ _____ _____

• *What insights do you have regarding the relationship between God's forgiveness and your emotional wholeness?*

_____

_____

Key #2: Saturate Yourself with Scripture

When you are forgiven, you have a clean slate before God, but it isn't enough to have a clean slate. You need to ask the Lord to write His truth on the slate of your heart. You need to have God's goodness instilled in you.

You acquire God's truth about virtually every situation by

reading His Word. You need to saturate yourself with God's opinion, and in the area of emotional health, that means saturating yourself with God's opinion about you.

In the Scriptures, you discover that you are

- *a child of God.* (See Gal. 3:26–27; 1 John 5:1–2.)
- *accepted totally and completely by God.* (See Acts 10:34–35; Eph. 1:3, 6.)
- *an heir of the Father through Christ Jesus.* (See Gal. 3:29; Titus 3:7.)

Many other descriptions of God's people appear in the Scriptures. You may want to start a list or circle them as you read your Bible daily. If you are born again into Christ Jesus, all of these descriptions about the children of God apply to you. Take them as part of your profile.

What the Word Says	What the Word Says to Me
For you are all sons of God through faith in Christ Jesus. For as many of you as were baptized into Christ have put on Christ (Gal. 3:26–27).	
Then Peter opened his mouth and said: "In truth I perceive that God shows no partiality. But in every nation whoever fears Him and works righteousness is accepted by Him" (Acts 10:34–35).	
Having been justified by His grace we should become heirs according to the hope of eternal life (Titus 3:7).	

- *What new insights do you have into your spiritual value to the Father? Can you see how these truths from God's Word can help build emotional wholeness in you?*

_____

_____

Key #3: Secure God's Healing for Your Faults

All people have something about themselves—their personalities, their backgrounds, their abilities—that they don't like. Everyone has a tendency to concentrate more on the flaws and points of weakness than on the strengths.

Some things in life are givens. For example, you can't change the family into which you were born, the nation in which you were born, your race, your physical stature and basic genetic code, and so forth. Certain physical weaknesses or disabilities cannot be changed. When you face these unchangeable things about yourself, you are wise to accept the way God made you. To do anything else is counterproductive. You need to assume God had a plan and purpose for every detail of your creation.

Some things in life are givens because of the state of the world in which you live. For example, you may not be able to do anything to alter the fact that your parents are divorced, or that your children are divorced. But you can pray that the Lord will bring about healing in you and in your loved ones.

In yet another area, elements of your personality *can* be changed. For example, you may think that you are jealous by nature. Let me assure you, envy is an acquired trait. You can ask the Lord to heal you of your jealousy and to help you to trust Him and, in your trust of Him, to trust others.

How do you become healed?

First, you identify the character or personality trait that you know is displeasing to the Lord and ask Him to forgive you for allowing this trait to develop.

Second, you ask Him to heal you of this tendency.

Third, you give Him permission to do whatever He needs to do in your life to make you whole.

Fourth, accept with your faith that God is at work in your life and that He will make you whole in His timing and according to His methods.

God is merciful. He forgives; He heals; He enters with His divine presence any area of your life that you open up to Him.

What the Word Says	What the Word Says to Me
Now may the God of peace Himself sanctify you completely; and may your whole spirit, soul, and body be preserved blameless at the coming of our Lord Jesus Christ. He who calls you is faithful, who also will do it (1 Thess. 5:23–24).	
Then I went down to the potter's house, and there he was, making something at the wheel. And the vessel that he made of clay was marred in the hand of the potter; so he made it again into another vessel, as it seemed good to the potter to make. Then the word of the LORD came to me, saying . . . "Can I not do with you as this potter?" says the LORD. "Look, as the clay is in the potter's hand, so are you in My hand"(Jer. 18:3–6).	

• *In what areas of your emotional life are you being challenged today to trust God to heal you?*

_____

_____

Key #4: Stop Bartering with God

Maybe you have an approach to God that can be stated like this: "If I just work hard enough and do enough good in my life, God will approve of me." You are attempting to barter good works for God's acceptance.

God accepts you! But you are having trouble accepting God's love.

You may have difficulty accepting the mercy of God because you have never fully received God's love. Or you may be so accustomed to the give-and-take, buy-and-sell nature of our culture that you assume you can deal with God the same way: "You do this for me and I'll do this for You." God doesn't operate according to that human principle.

God's principle is one of total acceptance of you when you ask for His forgiveness and seek to do His will. If He desires to change something in your life—always for your good and for your eventual blessing—His chastisement is patient and kind (never beyond your ability to bear), and His love is constant (never withheld or removed). You can't barter your way around God's will. Stop trying.

What should be your approach instead of bartering?

Trust God. Ask Him for what you desire, and then trust Him to answer your prayer according to His wisdom and infinite provision.

What the Word Says	What the Word Says to Me
We trust in the living God, who is the Savior of all men, espe-	_____ _____

cially of those who believe (1   _ _ _ _ _ _ _ _ _ _ _ _ _ _ _ _ _ _ _
Tim. 4:10).   _ _ _ _ _ _ _ _ _ _ _ _ _ _ _ _ _ _ _

Seek first the kingdom of God   _ _ _ _ _ _ _ _ _ _ _ _ _ _ _ _ _ _ _
and His righteousness, and all   _ _ _ _ _ _ _ _ _ _ _ _ _ _ _ _ _ _ _
these things shall be added to   _ _ _ _ _ _ _ _ _ _ _ _ _ _ _ _ _ _ _
you (Matt. 6:33).   _ _ _ _ _ _ _ _ _ _ _ _ _ _ _ _ _ _ _

I will leave in your midst   _ _ _ _ _ _ _ _ _ _ _ _ _ _ _ _ _ _ _
A meek and humble people,   _ _ _ _ _ _ _ _ _ _ _ _ _ _ _ _ _ _ _
And they shall trust in the name   _ _ _ _ _ _ _ _ _ _ _ _ _ _ _ _ _ _ _
of the LORD (Zeph. 3:12).   _ _ _ _ _ _ _ _ _ _ _ _ _ _ _ _ _ _ _

- *In what ways are you being challenged today to trust God for all that you need, especially in the areas of emotional love, support, and wholeness?*

Key #5: Share Yourself with Others

Too much introspection into your problems and weaknesses can cause you to become ingrown. Have you ever had an ingrown toenail? Then you know how just a small ingrown element of your physical body can cause pain. This same principle applies to your spiritual and emotional lives. You can turn inward and over time cause great damage to yourself, all in the name of trying to know yourself or fix your problems.

The best cure for many emotional difficulties is to turn outward to others and start giving of yourself to others. You may say, "But I don't have anything to give." Every person has something to give, even if it's only a smile, a kind word, or a pat on the shoulder in a time of need. Sometimes just your presence can be a gift to someone, especially to someone who is lonely, grieving, or suffering with a long-standing illness.

The happiest people I know are those who have wide-open hearts and who give generously to others. Such individuals are totally secure in God's love.

Give without any expectation of receiving from the person to whom you give. God will see your heart and what you do and reward you accordingly. Trust Him to take care of you.

By giving freely and generously, you open up yourself. This open stance before God and other people is important to emotional health. It is only as you open yourself that you learn to trust, and being able to trust is vital to your ability to receive God's forgiveness and healing, and to believe that God will supply your needs.

What the Word Says	What the Word Says to Me
You will keep him in perfect	_____
peace,	_____
Whose mind is stayed on You,	_____
Because he trusts in You.	_____
Trust in the LORD forever,	_____
For in YAH, the LORD, is ever-	_____
lasting strength (Isa. 26:3–4).	_____
Then Peter said, "Silver and gold	_____
I do not have, but what I do have	_____
I give you: In the name of Jesus	_____
Christ of Nazareth, rise up and	_____
walk." And he took him by the	_____
right hand and lifted him up,	_____
and immediately his feet and an-	_____
kle bones received strength. So	_____
he, leaping up, stood and walked	_____
and entered the temple with	_____
them—walking, leaping, and	_____
praising God. And all the people	_____

were filled with wonder and
amazement at what had happened (Acts 3:6–10).

_____

_____

_____

• *What new insights do you have about the importance of giving to emotional health?*

_____

_____

• *In what ways are you feeling challenged to become a more giving person?*

_____

_____

Key #6: Stop Dwelling on Your Past Failures

A part of receiving God's forgiveness is forgiving yourself. Once God has forgiven you, you have no claim to your past sins, failures, or weaknesses. You are a new creature in Christ Jesus!

Each time you dwell on your past failures and errors, you are closing, to a certain degree, your heart and mind to the current and future blessing that God has for you. Force yourself to think instead of the many ways God has helped you and blessed you. Anytime you find yourself reflecting on past failures, remind yourself that God has delivered you from sin. You have been saved by Christ Jesus. You are forgiven!

Then turn your mind to the positive things that God has done for you, in you, and through you. Start praising Him for His goodness.

What the Word Says

What the Word Says to Me

For You, LORD, are most high
above all the earth;

_____

_____

You are exalted far above all
gods. . . .
He preserves the souls of His
saints;
He delivers them out of the hand
of the wicked.
Light is sown for the righteous,
And gladness for the upright in
heart.
Rejoice in the LORD, you righteous,
And give thanks at the remem-
brance of His holy name (Ps.
97:9–12).

Let us search out and examine
our ways,
And turn back to the LORD;
Let us lift our hearts and hands
To God in heaven (Lam. 3:40–
41).

- *What new insights do you have into the ways in which a negative
  attitude toward your past failures and sins can keep you emotionally stunted?*

- *In what ways are you being challenged by the Lord?*

Key #7: Ask the Holy Spirit for Help

The Holy Spirit is imparted to you when you place your trust in Jesus Christ. The ministry of the Holy Spirit is to give you daily guidance and counsel—in other words, to help you walk in the ways of the Lord and to make wise choices as various situations and circumstances arise.

Ask for the help of the Holy Spirit on a daily basis. Ask Him to guard you from evil and to guide you into righteousness. Give Him charge over your agenda, your schedule, and your daily appointments. Trust Him to bring you to persons in need so that you might minister to them, and to bring to you the help you need in the form that is best for you to receive it.

What the Word Says	What the Word Says to Me
[Jesus said,] "I will pray the Father, and He will give you another Helper, that He may abide with you forever—the Spirit of truth, whom the world cannot receive, because it neither sees Him nor knows Him; but you know Him, for He dwells with you and will be in you" (John 14:16–17).	_____ _____ _____ _____ _____ _____ _____ _____
[Jesus said,] "And when He has come, He will convict the world of sin, and of righteousness, and of judgment" (John 16:8).	_____ _____ _____ _____

- *What new insights do you have into your emotional health and how to put yourself into a position to be made whole by God?*

_____

_____

THE ACHE OF ANXIETY

Our world is filled with anxious people. It doesn't seem to matter in which profession or area they work—ecology, economy, politics, parenting—people are anxious about the future, unseen dangers, personal status and approval, their health, and their general ability to work and succeed in life. Many are anxious about the state of their souls and whether they are in right standing with God. Even Christians have these concerns.

In the Sermon on the Mount, Jesus dealt with anxiety more than any other topic:

So why do you worry about clothing? Consider the lilies of the field, how they grow: they neither toil nor spin; and yet I say to you that even Solomon in all his glory was not arrayed like one of these. Now if God so clothes the grass of the field, which today is, and tomorrow is thrown into the oven, will He not much more clothe you, O you of little faith? Therefore do not worry, saying, "What shall we eat?" or "What shall we drink?" or "What shall we wear?" For after all these things the Gentiles seek. For your heavenly Father knows that you need all these things. But seek first the kingdom of God and His righteousness, and all these things shall be added to you. Therefore do not worry about tomorrow, for tomorrow will worry about its own things. Sufficient for the day is its own trouble (Matt. 6:28–34).

The words *anxious* and *anxiety* aren't found in the Greek. Usually, we find the word *worry*, such as in this version: "Do not worry." The concept of anxiety, however, is found throughout the New Testament. In Greek the word *merimna* is generally used; it means "to take thought." Issues such as these that Jesus raised aren't even to enter our minds, but if they do, we are to give them no lodging. That is, "Don't give it a second thought," or "It isn't worth thinking about."

And yet, how many of us spend anxious moments pondering what we will eat, drink, or wear, or how we will meet other daily practical and material needs in our lives? After all, food, drink, and clothing are some of our most basic needs. And that is the point that Jesus is making: God knows our basic needs. He is capable of meeting them, and He desires to meet them.

- *How do you feel when you are anxious?*

  _____

  _____

- *In your past experience, what have been the consequences of your experiencing anxiety?*

  _____

  _____

The Attitude of Anxiety

An attitude of anxiety goes beyond moments of feeling anxious from time to time. When an attitude of anxiety begins to rule our lives, our emotional well-being is in jeopardy.

Anxiety involves being pulled in two directions. It is an inner war. We are faced with choices about which direction to go or which consequence might occur (and therefore which one deserves our preparation and anticipation). We have a divided mind and also a certain degree of fear that we may make the wrong choice.

Anxiety is rarely a product of our environment. Certain circumstances don't automatically result in anxiety. What causes anxiety in some people doesn't affect other people at all. To a great extent, anxiety is a matter of attitude.

Let's consider the issue of speaking before groups of people. Some people delight in public speaking. Other people cringe at the very thought. If they think they have to speak to several people—even in a small group—their palms get clammy, their heads spin, they feel nauseous, and they start looking for an exit door. Anxiety takes over.

Public speaking, in and of itself, does not produce anxiety. Rather, the consequences a person perceives related to public speaking create anxiety.

Often people try to blame certain events, people, or situations for their anxiety. But anxiety lies within. It is an emotional response to a situation that can be controlled through the exercise of the will.

In an earlier lesson, I mentioned that every emotional response to life has a positive and negative side. On the positive side, a little anxiety can motivate us to action. If we awaken to find that we forgot to set the alarm and we are on the verge of being late to work, the anxiety can cause us to hurry a little to get to work on time.

On the negative side, however, is the possibility of deep-seated despair. When anxiety is allowed to build or develop into a pattern in our lives, it can be devastating.

- *What new insights do you have into the emotion of anxiety?*

_____

_____

Three Causes of Anxiety

There are at least three major causes of anxiety:

1. People perceive that they won't be able to meet or resolve their needs.

Jesus addressed this cause of anxiety in the Sermon on the Mount. Around A.D. 30 when Jesus preached this truth, the Hebrew people, for the most part, were living in poverty. The Romans drained the wealth of the land through taxation and acquisition. There were no social welfare programs as we know them today. People were consumed with the daily activity of earning enough just to meet the basic needs: food, shelter, and clothing.

Today, this cause of anxiety might be worry that people won't be able to pay the bills, find or keep a job, or provide sufficiently for their families. The causes of anxiety at this level are very real, practical, and material.

2. People set standards that can't be met, resulting in repeated failure and frustration. Much of this anxiety is rooted in intangible expectations, ideas, dreams, or self-set goals. Sometimes unrealistic standards are set by others—such as supervisors, parents, or spouses—but when that is the case, the response is usually not anxiety as much as it is anger or resentment. Only if people internalize the unrealistic expectations of others does anxiety take over.

Perfectionists struggle with this type of anxiety. Some people set standards for themselves that are far higher than those set by God! They expect absolute perfection in everything they do as well as everything others do.

3. People have unresolved hostility. When people feel anger, bitterness, or resentment over a period of time against a particular person, institution, or circumstance, they feel a constant agitation or irritation in their spirits. Again, this cause of anxiety is internal.

Now, just because anxiety is rooted in high expectations or unresolved hostility does not mean that it is any less real than anxiety rooted in the meeting of basic material needs. The anxiety is real, it is just as damaging, and it has the same hallmarks.

- *In your past experience, have you felt anxiety of these three types? What did you do?*

Signs of Anxiety

Proverbs 12:25 tells us, "Anxiety in the heart of man causes depression." In the King James Version, this verse reads, "Heaviness in the heart of man maketh it stoop." Anxiety pulls us down.

The symptoms associated with anxiety vary from person to person, but they generally involve one or more of these characteristics:

- Forgetfulness
- Inability to concentrate
- Irritability
- Inability to cope with small problems
- Vacillation in making decisions
- Misjudging other people
- Feeling persecuted
- Procrastination
- Gnawing dissatisfaction

These symptoms have dire consequences if they continue unchecked. Some consequences include the following:

- A feeling of drudgery about life, especially toward work and tasks
- A loss of excitement and enthusiasm
- A loss of productivity, creativity, and energy
- Damage to the physical body

In other words, nothing good comes from anxiety!

Jesus referred to some of the negative results of anxiety in a parable He taught:

Therefore hear the parable of the sower: When anyone hears the word of the kingdom, and does not understand it, then the wicked one comes and snatches away what was sown in his heart. This is he who received seed by the wayside. But he who received the seed on stony places, this is he who hears the word and immediately receives it with joy; yet he has no root in himself, but endures only for a while. For when tribulation or persecution arises because of the word, immediately he stumbles. Now he who received seed among the thorns is he who hears the word, and the cares of this world and the deceitfulness of riches choke the word, and he becomes unfruitful. But he who received seed on the good ground is he who hears the word and understands it, who indeed bears fruit and produces: some a hundredfold, some sixty, some thirty (Matt. 13:18–23).

The "cares of this world" choke off the productivity of a good seed sown in our lives. When we allow ourselves to become enveloped in anxiety, we become almost immune to any positive word, expression of faith, or insight from God.

If you are anxious, you are so overwhelmed in looking at your problems that you don't even think about what you might pursue as solutions. When that happens, the Word has very little impact in your life, which eliminates the very thing that can build faith and counteract anxiety. The spiral is a downward one.

Have you ever tried to read your Bible only to find that you've gone through several verses and don't have any recollection of what you have read? Chances are, anxiety was at work. You were seeing the words with your eyes, but other cares and concerns kept you from taking in the words of Scripture.

Note that Jesus taught this parable about the kingdom of God. He said that the "wicked one" snatches away some of the seed planted in our lives. But that isn't the case with anxiety. We are the ones who control what we will be anxious about. We are the ones who allow ourselves to worry.

If you have a loss of interest in life—a loss of enthusiasm, a loss of productivity and energy, a loss of output—consider whether you have developed an attitude of anxiety. If so, it's up to you to take action to break the hold that worry has over you. God will help you, but you must face what you have allowed to develop in your life and take action to counteract your response of worry and anxiety.

In what ways are you feeling challenged today about anxiety?

_____

_____

God's Answer to Anxiety

There are no easy-way-out solutions for people who have allowed anxiety to become a mind-set. They literally need to take hold of their minds and corral them, refusing to let anxiety reign.

Some people seek to escape anxiety. They turn to drugs, alcohol, or a change in geography in hopes of relieving their deep feelings of anxiety. Others go on wanton sprees of seeking pleasure or of buying items they don't really need. In all of these behaviors, they seek to substitute something for anxiety other than the peace of Jesus Christ.

These so-called solutions only add to the problem of anxiety. They may mask the problem for a while, but anxiety continues to brew and build. Eventually, people *must* deal with anxiety or face a serious mental, emotional, relational, or physical breakdown. When that time comes—and it inevitably comes—they face a mountain of anxiety and the problem of a possible addiction to the drugs, alcohol, or behavior sought as a solution.

You must deal with anxiety at its root. And what is that root? A failure to trust God.

At the foundation of anxiety is the belief that either God can't take care of the situation, or God won't—and either way, you lose because God doesn't act.

The only real lasting and healing solution for an attitude of anxiety is to place your trust in God.

1. Turn your heart over to God. If your relationship is wrong with God, you can't be right in yourself. If you are cut off from God's peace, you ultimately can have no peace.

If you are a Christian, you must come to God and confess to Him that you have failed to trust Him completely. Ask Him to forgive you for trying to continue to live your life according to your own plans, abilities, agendas, and talents. Receive His forgiveness, and ask the Holy Spirit to help you trust God with your whole heart, mind, and soul.

You may need to confess this to God many times in your life. The process is one of trusting Him more and more.

What the Word Says	What the Word Says to Me
He who dwells in the secret place	_____
of the Most High	_____
Shall abide under the shadow of	_____
the Almighty.	_____
I will say of the LORD, "He is my	_____
refuge and my fortress;	_____
My God, in Him I will trust" (Ps.	_____
91:1–2).	_____
In You, O LORD, I put my trust;	_____
Let me never be ashamed;	_____
Deliver me in Your righteous-	_____
ness.	_____
Bow down Your ear to me,	_____
Deliver me speedily;	_____
Be my rock of refuge,	_____
A fortress of defense to save me	_____
(Ps. 31:1–2).	_____

- *What new insights do you have about dealing with anxiety by trusting God?*

  _____

  _____

2. Tell God about how you feel. Something very beneficial comes from admitting to God the anxiety that you feel.

A verse admonishes you to "be anxious for nothing." This

phrase is followed by a call to prayer: "But in everything by prayer and supplication, with thanksgiving, let your requests be made known to God" (Phil. 4:6). The antidote for moments of anxiety is prayer—a conversation with God. Supplication refers to making petitions before God, asking Him specifically for what you desire. You are to accompany the prayer and supplication with thanksgiving; you are to give thanks even before you receive God's provision for the answer that you know is on the way!

How can you know that God's answer is coming to you? Because God is faithful to His Word. He loves you as His child and provides for you. In giving thanks, you are giving voice to the trust you are placing in God to love you and care for you.

What is the result of this kind of prayer? The next verse in Philippians says that after you have made known your requests to God, "The peace of God, which surpasses all understanding, will guard your [heart] and [mind] through Christ Jesus" (Phil. 4:7).

Through prayer, you *become* anxious for nothing and have the true peace of God ruling your heart instead of worry and its related frustrations and damaging effects.

What the Word Says	What the Word Says to Me
[Jesus said,] "Peace I leave with you, My peace I give to you; not as the world gives do I give to you. Let not your heart be troubled, neither let it be afraid" (John 14:27).	_____ _____ _____ _____ _____ _____
Let the peace of God rule in your hearts, to which also you were called in one body; and be thankful. Let the word of Christ dwell in you richly in all wisdom, teaching and admonishing one	_____ _____ _____ _____ _____

another in psalms and hymns
and spiritual songs, singing with
grace in your hearts to the Lord.
And whatever you do in word or
deed, do all in the name of the
Lord Jesus, giving thanks to God
the Father through Him (Col.
3:15–17).

_____

_____

_____

_____

_____

_____

_____

3. Turn the anxiety-causing problem over to God. After you have
prayed about your anxiety and the problem that gave rise to it,
leave your problem with God. As the old saying goes, "Let go and
let God."

That is what Peter meant when he wrote, "Casting all your care
upon Him, for He cares for you" (1 Peter 5:7). Trusting God to
solve your problem or meet your need means that you give the
problem to God 100 percent. Give Him *all* of your concern,
anxiety, worry.

Walk away, saying in your spirit, "I may not know how the
answer will come, and I may not know when, where, through
whom, or by what means. But I know the One who has the answer,
and I put my trust in Him."

What the Word Says

I found trouble and sorrow.
Then I called upon the name of
the LORD:
"O LORD, I implore You, deliver
my soul!"
Gracious is the LORD, and righteous;
Yes, our God is merciful.
The LORD preserves the simple;

What the Word Says to Me

_____

_____

_____

_____

_____

_____

_____

_____

I was brought low, and He saved me.
Return to your rest, O my soul,
For the LORD has dealt bountifully with you (Ps. 116:3–7).

Call to Me, and I will answer you, and show you great and mighty things, which you do not know (Jer. 33:3).

_____
_____
_____
_____
_____

_____
_____
_____
_____

4. Turn your mind to the positive blessings of God. Choose to think about something other than your problem. Choose to dwell on answers, solutions, hopes, dreams, goals, new ideas and opportunities, and good things of all types. Recall the many promises of God to you as His child. Search through your Bible and underscore passages of Scripture that speak of God's blessings, provision, and peace. (Use a concordance to find as many verses as you can.)

The mind concentrating on God's presence and work in this world has no room or time to dwell on evil, problems, or negative situations. The mind concentrating on God's goodness results in emotions of anticipation, hope, faith, and joy. Such an emotional state is the very opposite of anxiety and worry.

When Paul advised the Philippians to be anxious for nothing, and then told them to pray and give supplication to God with thanksgiving, promising them God's peace, his very next words encouraged the Philippians to meditate on praiseworthy things. (See Phil. 4:8.) His advice is for you today! So much of the world is steeped in bad news. How important it is for you to be steeped in even greater quantities of good news.

Direct your reading, your media watching, and your conversations to what is good. Discuss with others how the Lord is working in your life—how He is healing you, strengthening you, and bringing you to a higher plane in your spiritual life. Share with others the testimonies of people you know. Build up your faith and the faith of others.

When you have a positive, praiseworthy, optimistic, faith-filled approach to life, anxiety-causing situations will not affect you nearly as much as when you have a negative, down-in-the dumps, God-has-forgotten-me attitude. Your best approach to prevent anxiety is to concentrate on the praiseworthy and to voice your praise to God. Make abundant praise a daily part of your prayer life.

What the Word Says	What the Word Says to Me
I will praise You with my whole heart . . .	_____
I will sing praises to You.	_____
I will worship toward Your holy temple,	_____
And praise Your name	_____
For Your lovingkindness and Your truth;	_____
For You have magnified Your word above all Your name.	_____
In the day when I cried out, You answered me,	_____
And made me bold with strength in my soul (Ps. 138:1–3).	_____

- *What new insights do you have into the nature of anxiety and how to find emotional healing for anxiety in trusting God?*

  _____

  _____

- *In what ways do you feel challenged today to be free of anxiety?*

  _____

  _____

LESSON 7

THE GRIP OF FEAR

Fear is one of the most potent emotions we can feel. It is our number one natural defense against all things that are harmful to us.

Everybody is afraid of *something*. I defy any person to come face-to-face with a shark, a coiled and hissing rattlesnake, or a grizzly bear and *not* feel fear.

The disciples of Jesus experienced fear:

> Immediately Jesus made His disciples get into the boat and go before Him to the other side, while He sent the multitudes away. And when He had sent the multitudes away, He went up on the mountain by Himself to pray. Now when evening came, He was alone there. But the boat was now in the middle of the sea, tossed by the waves, for the wind was contrary. Now in the fourth watch of the night Jesus went to them, walking on the sea. And when the disciples saw Him walking on the sea, they were troubled, saying, "It is a ghost!" And they cried out for fear. But immediately Jesus spoke to them saying, "Be of good cheer! It is I; do not be afraid" (Matt. 14:22–27).

The disciples were afraid of what they didn't perceive fully, and they were afraid of what they thought had the potential to hurt or destroy them. That is the nature of fear: we fear what we don't know, and we fear what we think will hurt us.

- *Have you ever been afraid of what you didn't know?*

_____

_____

- *Can you recall a time when you were afraid of something that you believed could cause you injury or harm?*

_____

_____

Types of Good Fear

Fear comes in two varieties—good, health-related, safety-related, positive fear, and negative, damaging fear.

We *should* fear some things.

We should have a healthy fear of the Lord. You may want to think of this type of fear as reverence or awe. When we encounter the Lord, we come into the presence of the sovereign King of the universe.

Although the Lord certainly has the power to destroy, and we cannot ever fully understand or know the Lord, the fear that we feel about the judgment of God must be balanced with our awe that God is all-loving and ever merciful to us, His children. Our fear of God is a healthy fear to have. It is the awe of humble children before an awesome Father.

Adam and Eve had a fear of God after they sinned in the Garden of Eden, and they hid themselves.

Ever since then, men and women have been responding as Adam and Eve did. When we fear God, we attempt to hide from Him. We run from God, or we try to convince ourselves that He doesn't exist.

- *Have you ever had an experience of attempting to hide from God?*

_____

_____

• *How did you feel while you were hiding?*

_____

_____

The only solution for this fear that results from sin is to face God and to admit that we are afraid, we've been running, and we have sinned.

Adam and Eve didn't do that. They attempted to justify what they had done—placing the blame on someone else. We have no mention of Adam and Eve's owning up to their sin or seeking God's forgiveness. As a result, they faced God's chastisement.

If you are afraid of God today because of a sin that you believe you have committed, come to the Father and own up to that sin, accept what Jesus did on the cross in providing a sacrifice for your sin, and ask God for forgiveness.

A healthy fear of God brings you to a position of praise and worship, and also of heeding God's commandments. As you read through the verses below, identify the positive benefits of a healthy fear of the Lord.

What the Word Says	What the Word Says to Me
Who shall not fear You, O Lord, and glorify Your name? For You alone are holy. For all nations shall come and worship before You, For Your judgments have been manifested (Rev. 15:4).	
The fear of the LORD is the beginning of knowledge, But fools despise wisdom and instruction (Prov. 1:7).	

Come and hear, all you who fear
God,
And I will declare what He has
done for my soul (Ps. 66:16).

_____
_____
_____
_____

- *Have you ever been afraid of God?*

_____

_____

- *What new insights do you have into the fear of the Lord?*

_____

_____

We should have a healthy fear of sin. Sin has the power to destroy our lives, not only to cause great damage to us today, but also to affect our eternal destiny. When we fear sin, we fear sin's consequences, which are deadly.

Many people dismiss lightly the nature of sin. In part, they do this because we all sin, and they have a false notion that if everybody is doing it, it must be all right. In part, they deny the power of sin because they *hope* that God might overlook the sin, and thus, the sin will have no consequences. Both lines of thinking are 100 percent wrong.

Sin is never overlooked by God, and it never goes unpunished. God's Word defines very clearly the nature of sin and the nature of righteousness, and it declares very strongly that the consequence for unrepented, unforgiven sin is ultimately eternal death.

What the Word Says

For the wages of sin is death, but the gift of God is eternal life in Christ Jesus our Lord (Rom. 6:23).

What the Word Says to Me

_____
_____
_____
_____

Let us lay aside every weight, and the sin which so easily en-snares us (Heb. 12:1).

_____

_____

_____

* *In what ways are you being challenged today to fear sin?*

_____

_____

We should have a healthy fear of Satan, the enemy of our souls. Jesus said that Satan is a thief who has the power to steal, kill, and destroy. (See John 10:10.) He is a formidable enemy, stronger than we are but weaker than Christ Jesus. Only as we live in right standing with the Father (through the redemptive work of Christ), seek to live out the will of God for our lives, and use the name of Jesus do we have authority to resist the devil and overcome him.

Too many Christians speak too lightly of the devil. They treat him as if he is a human enemy that can be defeated handily. The Scriptures give us a much different portrayal of the enemy of our souls. They tell us that Satan is the father of all lies and deception, the master manipulator, the archenemy of God, the one who continually seeks to devour us as a roaring lion.

What the Word Says

He who sins is of the devil, for the devil has sinned from the be-ginning. For this purpose the Son of God was manifested, that He might destroy the works of the devil (1 John 3:8).

Be sober, be vigilant; because your adversary the devil walks about like a roaring lion, seeking

What the Word Says to Me

_____

_____

_____

_____

_____

_____

_____

_____

_____

whom he may devour. Resist
him, steadfast in the faith (1 Peter 5:8–9).

Put on the whole armor of God,
that you may be able to stand
against the wiles of the devil. For
we do not wrestle against flesh and
blood, but against principalities,
against powers, against the rulers
of the darkness of this age, against
spiritual hosts of wickedness in the
heavenly places (Eph. 6:11–12).

Other Types of Healthy Fear

In addition to a healthy fear of God, sin, and the devil, there are
other healthy fears. Every parent attempts to teach the child a fear
of touching a hot stove, running out in the street, and talking to
strangers. We seem to be born with a healthy fear of sudden loud
noises and of falling. It is natural to feel a moment of fear when
we hear an unusual sound outside the home or hear the sirens
warning of a tornado, flash flood, or hurricane. As stated earlier,
such fears motivate us to act.

What we need to do in the face of such fears is to act in a positive
manner. Our fear is healthy if we respond to a fear of sin by seeking
forgiveness for that sin and repenting (making a change in the will
not to commit the sin again). Our fear is healthy if we respond to
a fear of a hot stove by not touching a stove. Our fear is healthy if
we respond to a warning siren by seeking shelter.

Unhealthy Fear

When we respond in a negative manner, our fear is unhealthy.
Negative responses might include

- being paralyzed by fear, seemingly unable to move, react, or take evasive action.
- being frazzled by fear, moving in too many directions at once (or running in circles).
- being overwhelmed by fear, so that we choose a response of hiding from all of life.

The result of negative responses to fear is that we don't act in a way that can bring us relief from fear or bring us relief from whatever has caused our fear. In failing to move or act—and in failing to focus on a response—we place ourselves in continued danger and, therefore, in continued fear.

- *Have you ever had an experience of responding negatively to fear?*

_____

_____

- *What new insights do you have into the nature of healthy fear?*

_____

_____

- *How do you feel when you have healthy fear? Unhealthy fear?*

_____

_____

The Spiritual Impact of Unhealthy Fear

Healthy fear is for our protection, both in the natural and in the spiritual realms. An unhealthy fear, however, can be devastating. The apostle Paul warned Timothy of unhealthy fear: "I remind you to stir up the gift of God which is in you through the laying on of my hands. For God has not given us a spirit of fear, but of power and of love and of a sound mind" (2 Tim. 1:6–7).

An unhealthy fear diminishes us spiritually because when we are overwhelmed by fear we tend to

- fail to give a bold witness of Christ Jesus.
- fail to take risks in launching new ministry out-reaches.
- fail to respond fully to God's love.
- fail to grow in our faith.

Fear not only destroys; it demoralizes. It robs us of hope. And when we no longer have hope, we give in to despair, depression, and dejection. We lose an awareness of possibility, dreams, and goals.

- *Can you recall an experience in which fear kept you from proclaiming the good news of Christ Jesus?*

_____

_____

What the Word Says

I want you to know, brethren, that the things which happened to me have actually turned out for the furtherance of the gospel, so that it has become evident to the whole palace guard, and to all the rest, that my chains are in Christ; and most of the brethren in the Lord, having become confident by my chains, are much more bold to speak the word without fear (Phil. 1:12–14).

[Jesus said,] "If they have called the master of the house Beelzebub, how much more will they call those of his household! Therefore

What the Word Says to Me

_____

_____

_____

_____

_____

_____

_____

_____

_____

_____

_____

_____

_____

_____

_____

do not fear them. For there is
nothing covered that will not be
revealed, and hidden that will
not be known" (Matt. 10:25–26).

$$\text{_____}$$

Basic Fears That We Face

Every person faces certain fears that seem common not only to our present age, but also to all eras:

Poverty. We fear not having enough material substance. We fear losing our jobs or sources of income. We fear bill collectors, creditors, and the possibility of bankruptcy. We fear financial failure.

Death. We fear the unknown "beyond."

Ill health. We fear losing our quality of life to illness or injury. We fear becoming incapacitated mentally or physically. We fear pain and suffering.

Loss of love. We fear the possibility of divorce, estrangement, and the loss of regular contact with loved ones. We fear parents dying and children leaving home. We fear those who might woo our loved ones away from us.

Old age. We fear being isolated and lonely. We fear losing our capacity to work and an increasing inability to do those things we did when we were young.

Criticism. We fear what others will think of us and say about us.

We can choose to respond positively to each fear. For example, we can do many things to keep ourselves healthy as we age. We can build retirement or savings plans to avert future poverty. We can stay interested in life, continue to learn new things, and work to strengthen friendships and family ties. We can inform ourselves more fully in areas where a lack of knowledge contributes to fear.

Or we can respond negatively to our fears. When we do, we nearly always visualize *potential* negative consequences, things that *might* happen, but that are not inevitable.

Some of what we imagine is an illusion. Even so, our bodies tend to react to negative, fearful imaginations as if what we are imagining is real.

This is especially true in the area of criticism. So many people are fearful of what others might think or say about them. They dread encounters and circumstances with certain people. As a result, they refuse to go to certain places or engage in certain activities that might be beneficial for them because they fear being ridiculed or otherwise criticized. The people they fear have a "hold" on their lives.

What the Word Says	What the Word Says to Me
The fear of man brings a snare, But whoever trusts in the LORD shall be safe (Prov. 29:25).	_____ _____ _____
Inasmuch then as the children have partaken of flesh and blood, He Himself likewise shared in the same, that through death He might destroy him who had the power of death, that is, the devil, and release those who through fear of death were all their lifetime subject to bondage (Heb. 2:14–15).	_____ _____ _____ _____ _____ _____ _____ _____
He Himself has said, "I will never leave you nor forsake you." So we may boldly say: "The LORD is my helper; I will not fear. What can man do to me?" (Heb. 13:5–6).	_____ _____ _____ _____ _____ _____

• *What do you tend to fear? How do you respond to those fears? What is the result?*

_____

_____

- *In what ways are you feeling challenged to confront your fears today?*

_____

_____

A Spirit of Fear

Negative fears—and an unhealthy response to fear—can result in a spirit of fear. This spirit of timidity keeps us from taking risks of love. It keeps us from reaching out to others, from revealing our innermost thoughts and feelings, from developing deep, satisfying relationships.

Fear that is not healed by God becomes a pervasive emotional response to all of life, whether it is meeting new people, pursuing new opportunities, facing challenges, or standing up against evil. When a spirit of fear takes hold, people are often unable to help themselves. They need loving friends to intercede in prayer on their behalf. They nearly always need wise counsel from a godly person.

- *In your experience, have you ever known someone who seemed to have a spirit of fear?*

_____

_____

Response to the Grip of Fear

Remember Paul's words to Timothy: God gives you a spirit of power and of love and of a sound mind. (See 2 Tim. 1:7.) Your response to every person or situation that you fear is God's power, God's love, and God's mind.

1. Ask for God's help. When you are struck with fear, your first response should be to ask for God's help. Avail yourself of the power of God.

At the beginning of this lesson, we read how Jesus walked on the sea to His disciples. Peter heard the Lord say, "Be of good cheer!" and he said,

> "Lord, if it is You, command me to come to You on the water." So He said, "Come." And when Peter had come down out of the boat, he walked on the water to go to Jesus. But when he saw that the wind was boisterous, he was afraid; and beginning to sink he cried out, saying, "Lord, save me!" And immediately Jesus stretched out His hand and caught him (Matt. 14:28–31).

When Peter found himself in trouble and fear—sinking in the sea—he had the right response. He asked for God's help. "Lord, save me!" is your best first response at any time you feel fear.

2. *Ask for God's love to fill your heart.* Love is a potent antidote for fear. I recall the first time I preached in my home church. I had a "fear attack"—after all, the people knew me. I felt they expected more from me than a group of strangers might expect. What helped me? I read the words of the Lord to Joshua in Joshua 1:5–9, and then I turned my focus on the people of my home church. I was overwhelmed by how much I loved them. The more I thought about how much I loved them and how they had loved me through the years, the more my fear evaporated. When I stood in the pulpit, the fear completely drained out of me, and I felt full of God's love, the power of His anointing, and the desire to preach God's Word.

John had a great deal to say about God's love—both in his gospel and in his letters to the church. We read in 1 John 4:17–18:

> Love has been perfected among us in this: that we may have boldness in the day of judgment; because as He is, so are we in this world. There is no fear in love; but perfect love casts out fear, because fear involves torment. But he who fears has not been made perfect in love.

Ask your heavenly Father to impart to you more of Christ's love and to take away any torment you feel. Let the perfect love of Jesus Christ flood your soul. As you do, fear will lose its grip on you.

3. *Ask God to give you a sound mind filled with and operating according to God's Word.* The basis for a sound mind is the Word of God. The more you know of God's promises to you, and the more you live according to His commandments and statutes, the greater your strength to withstand fear.

If you have memorized Isaiah 41:10, you can use it to speak directly to the source of your fear, just as Jesus quoted Scripture to the devil during His time of temptation in the wilderness. (Refer to Luke 4:1–13.)

What the Word Says	What the Word Says to Me
Fear not, for I am with you;	_____
Be not dismayed, for I am your	_____
God.	_____
I will strengthen you,	_____
Yes, I will help you,	_____
I will uphold you with My righ-	_____
teous right hand (Isa. 41:10).	_____
I will not leave you nor forsake	_____
you. Be strong and of good cour-	_____
age, for to this people you shall	_____
divide as an inheritance the land	_____
which I swore to their fathers to	_____
give them. Only be strong and	_____
very courageous, that you may	_____
observe to do according to all the	_____
law which Moses My servant	_____
commanded you; do not turn	_____
from it to the right hand or to	_____
the left, that you may prosper	_____

wherever you go. This Book of
the Law shall not depart from
your mouth, but you shall meditate in it day and night, that you
may observe to do according to
all that is written in it. For then
you will make your way prosper-
ous, and then you will have good
success. Have I not commanded
you? Be strong and of good courage; do not be afraid, nor be dis-
mayed, for the LORD your God is
with you wherever you go (Josh.
1:5–9).

When you are gripped by fear, turn your gaze upon God,
redirect your heart to love, speak to your fear from the Word of
God, and then respond boldly to the situation that caused your
fear. The Lord desires today that you "be strong and of good
courage."

- *What new insights do you have into the relationship between fear
  and emotional health?*

  _____

  _____

- *In what ways are you being challenged to deal with fear in your
  life?*

  _____

  _____

THE GRINDSTONE OF GUILT

Our entire nation seems to be under a cloud of guilt—a sense of past failure or error. We look around and see things not working in our personal lives, family lives, communities, and nation.

Guilt is like a giant weight on the heart and mind that slowly grinds down a person's enthusiasm, hope, and joy.

A serious detriment to the kingdom of God is a cloud of unworthiness that manifests itself in two ways:

1. Unworthiness to be used by God in various areas of witness, outreach, or ministry.

2. Unworthiness to receive God's abundant blessings.

Memories often come flooding back, along with a built-in guilt message, "And because of that, God can't use you," or "Because of your failure, God can't bless you." Guilt never allows you to forget what you once did.

Christians in many denominations have built a case against themselves that keeps them from receiving all that God has for them and from doing all that God desires for them to do. Their lack of self-value stalls the work of the Lord in the world.

- *How does guilt make you feel?*

_____

_____

- *Can you recall a time when guilt kept you (or may have kept you) from taking action for the Lord or receiving the Lord's blessing?*

Guilt is the fear of being found out and being punished for a sin or mistake. We all experience guilt at some point because we all sin, we all err, we all make mistakes. The question is not whether we experience guilt, but how we deal with it.

Forgiveness Is the Remedy for Guilt

Forgiveness is the remedy for guilt. A sense of guilt about one's sinful nature is often a factor in a person's coming to Christ.

Let me remind you of several things about God's forgiveness as we deal with this issue of guilt:

Full provision for forgiveness has already been provided by God for all persons, prior to their asking for forgiveness or accepting it. Jesus died on the cross as the perfect, complete, and only sacrifice necessary to free every person from sin.

You don't need to plead for forgiveness or try to impress God that you are worthy to be forgiven. You need to accept and *receive* what God has provided through His Son, Jesus Christ. When you ask for forgiveness, God freely and unconditionally grants it. (See 1 John 1:9.)

Furthermore, you can't do anything that will impress God to forgive you on the basis of your merits. His blameless, sinless, perfect Son has already died on your behalf. What more could you possibly do? You don't need to die on a cross to be forgiven. Even if you did so, you aren't a perfect, sinless person. Nothing short of Christ's death is acceptable to God as a reason for you to be forgiven. No amount of works or charitable deeds will qualify you for God's free offer of salvation through Christ Jesus. (See Eph. 2:8–9.)

God's forgiveness is not automatic, however. You must accept or receive it. You do this by coming to your heavenly Father in humility, admitting that you are a sinner in need of forgiveness, acknowledging that Jesus Christ died on the cross on your behalf, and believing that what He did provides the means of forgiveness for you. Some people call this an act of confession.

You may question why you need to do this if God has already forgiven you. The purpose is that you might know with certainty in your heart that you are forgiven and then experience the cleansing power of forgiveness.

The aftermath of receiving God's forgiveness is to repent—which literally means to change your mind—for your past sins and to make a new choice to follow in the footsteps of Jesus and live according to God's commandments and statutes. The ability to follow through on this new commitment to right living before the Father comes from the indwelling power and presence of the Holy Spirit, who joins with your spirit at the time you receive God's forgiveness and accept Jesus Christ as your Savior and Lord.

Thus, God forgives you from past sins, and He enables you *not* to sin in the future. (See 1 John 5:18.)

Have you taken these steps to receive God's forgiveness in your life? If not, I invite you to do so today.

What the Word Says	What the Word Says to Me

For by grace you have been saved through faith, and that not of yourselves; it is the gift of God, not of works, lest anyone should boast (Eph. 2:8–9).

If we say that we have no sin, we deceive ourselves, and the truth is not in us. If we confess our sins, He is faithful and just to forgive us our sins and to cleanse us from all unrighteousness (1 John 1:8–9).

We know that whoever is born of
God does not sin; but he who has
been born of God keeps himself,
and the wicked one does not
touch him (1 John 5:18).

You may say to me, "Do you mean that once I have accepted Christ, I will never experience guilt again?"

No, what I'm saying is that a sin nature produces in a person a state of guilt. The person who has never turned to God and received His forgiveness has a perpetual underlying guilt that she can never escape. The person may harden her heart to the point that it *seems* she no longer feels guilty for her sin, but deep inside, during dark, life-and-death moments, she knows that she is estranged from God and feels her sin and its related guilt. Sin doesn't exist without its emotional counterpart, guilt.

When you accept Christ as your personal Savior and Lord, you are freed from the state of sin and guilt. From time to time you may sin, and when that happens, the Holy Spirit brings a conviction that a wrong has been committed before the Father. Guilt is the warning bell that sin has taken place. Guilt should be the signal for you to go to the Father and say, "I have sinned. Please cleanse me of this, and help me never to do this again."

You may be slow in responding to guilt. You allow guilt to build up. Then you may fall into one of these traps:

- "I'm a Christian who should have known better. I don't see how God can forgive me."
- "I keep committing this same sin. God is not going to forgive me this time."
- "God knows my weakness, and since He hasn't changed this part of me, He must know that I'm going to continue to sin in this way."
- "I've waited too long to ask for God's forgiveness."

All of these lines of reasoning are in error. God always stands ready to forgive you when you come to Him with a contrite heart.

When you sin, you must go *immediately* to your loving heavenly Father and ask Him to cleanse you, renew you, and help you not to sin further.

- *Have you had times when you felt guilt for sins you had committed? What did you do? What were the results?*

_____

_____

Three Types of Guilt

Guilt is guilt, but the direction of guilt tends to fall into one of these three categories:

1. Guilt toward God. You feel guilty because you have never sought God's forgiveness, or as a Christian, you have sinned against God.

2. Guilt toward others. You feel guilty because you have sinned against another person.

3. Guilt toward yourself (false guilt). False guilt occurs when you manufacture a feeling of guilt for something that you erroneously assume you have done, or for something in which you feel you have had a part.

For example, a young woman may feel guilty for having been the victim of incest, rape, or sexual abuse. Even though she is an innocent victim, she falsely assumes that because she was involved in a sinful act, she bears responsibility for the sin. Or she may feel that she did something to bring about the sin or contribute to it. She feels guilt even though before God, she is innocent.

Or a young man may apply for a job and get it, unaware that his friend applied for the same job earlier. He feels as if he has betrayed his friend. Before God, he is innocent, yet he feels guilty.

Many people carry false guilt with them from their childhood days. They feel guilty for their parents' divorce, the illness of a grandparent, the injury to a sibling—even though they were not remotely responsible for what transpired.

False guilt is just as real as guilt for sins against God and guilt for sins against others. It feels the same, and it bears the same consequences. The difference is, false guilt ends up being directed at yourself, and false guilt is *not* directly linked to sin. False guilt is guilt without sin.

All three types of guilt are bad. Nothing good comes from unresolved guilt.

- *In your past, have you (or someone you know) experienced false guilt? What did you do? What were the results?*

_____

_____

Results of Guilt

A load of guilt has many behavioral manifestations in a person's life. These are among them:

A refusal to succeed. A person suffering with guilt tends to undermine his own success, feeling unworthy of success in the light of what he has done.

A low energy level. Guilt saps energy. The mind continues to be weighed down with memories of the sin committed (or in which she believes she has participated). The person doesn't exhibit the ambition or fortitude to move forward or to attempt new challenges.

A loss of joy and peace. The guilty person doesn't know deep, inner contentment. He feels frustrated. There is a restlessness in the spirit and emotions until forgiveness is received.

Self-punishment. Feeling of little use and unworthy of blessing, the guilty person often tries to punish herself. In some cases, she does this to try to avert what she believes would be God's punishment.

Feelings of insecurity. The guilty person who has sinned against God feels insecure in his relationship with God. The one who has sinned against another person feels insecure in his relationship with that person. The person who suffers from false guilt tends to feel insecure in a general sense.

Physical problems. Guilt carried for long periods of time weighs down and grinds away at the heart and mind, and eventually that grinding stone seems to affect the physical body. Feeling unworthy, the guilty person readily engages in physically negative behaviors—addictions, excesses, and a general failure to be concerned about health.

Increased "works, works, works." The guilty person sometimes displays a burst of activity that she hopes will be perceived as good—a heavy dose of charitable or voluntary goodness to balance the sin committed. This is false recompense because it doesn't involve genuine forgiveness from God or others.

Lack of interest in prayer or involvement in ministry activities. The guilty person doesn't think God will hear him, bless him, or respond to him and therefore doesn't attempt to communicate with God.

The ultimate consequence of guilt, of course, is that a person is in danger of losing his soul. The more a person shuts himself off from God and other Christians, the more he isolates himself from forgiveness and wholeness. The resulting state is misery and isolation. The person goes into hiding from the world.

If you are carrying a load of guilt today, you need to recognize that you may wear a mask that is effective in hiding your guilt from others, but you cannot stop its deadly and potentially eternal consequences from occurring on the inside. You need to respond to the guilt by facing your sin and owning up to it, and then seek and receive God's forgiveness and the forgiveness of others you may have wronged. If you are carrying a load of false guilt, you need to come to grips with the truth of your situation.

- *What insights do you have into the nature of sin and guilt and the resulting consequences?*

———————————————————————

———————————————————————

• *In what ways are you feeling challenged today regarding guilt?*

_____

_____

Steps for Being Free of Guilt

We have touched on several of the key steps required to be free of guilt, all under the banner of forgiveness. These steps are summarized below.

1. Face up to the sin that resulted in your guilt. Admit your sin to God. If you have sinned against another person, confess to that person that you have sinned against him or her.

In facing up to your sin, make certain that it is a sin before God. The sin you think you have committed may have been a mistake or error or somebody else's sin.

Mistake or error. Unless you have done something willful to rebel against God's Word or to breach your relationship with God and other people, you likely have made a mistake or error. You certainly can apologize for mistakes and errors. You can ask God to help you not to repeat the same errors. You can commit yourself to a new start. Some things that we call sin aren't sin.

On the other hand, our society is quick to dismiss some behaviors that are against God's Word as normal. The Bible presents a very clear picture of what is sin and what isn't. If you have any doubt about whether you have sinned, consult the Scriptures.

Somebody else's sin. Own up to whatever role you think you played in a sinful event, but don't assume blame for something that wasn't your fault. You may be wise to consult someone who can give you godly counsel about whether you have fault in a situation. Make sure the advice is in line with the Scriptures.

When you confess to God or a person that you have sinned against him, don't try to justify what you did. Simply state your sin or error. And then ask God or the person to forgive you.

2. Make amends. If you have wronged another person, don't

merely try to substitute a request for forgiveness by doing kind deeds for the person. This same principle holds for your relationship with God. Don't try to substitute works for genuine forgiveness.

In seeking to make amends for a wrong committed against another person, you may be wise to ask the person what she would consider to be a fair compensation for the hurt or injury, or you may want to offer compensation of some type. Or the best compensation may be a genuine change in your life (which may involve counseling or professional help or therapy). Ask God to give you wisdom in identifying appropriate amends. Also ask Him to give you the courage and the fortitude to follow through on your commitment to the offended person and to yourself.

3. *Accept forgiveness*. If you have sinned against God and have repented, you can be assured that He forgives you. His Word promises that He will, and God is always faithful to His Word.

If you have sinned against another person and he forgives you, accept his words of forgiveness at face value. Don't try to second-guess his sincerity or motives.

What happens if you confess a sin against another person and the person refuses to forgive you? She bears the responsibility for failing to forgive; you don't. You have done what the Lord requires of you, and you stand clear before the Lord.

What about false guilt? Tell God about it. Ask Him to erase from you all feelings of guilt and to heal you of any damage the false guilt may have caused in your life. Ask Him to help you to forgive yourself fully for any participation in a sinful activity or incident and to move forward in your life.

The verses of Scripture below relate to guilt, confession, and forgiveness. Keep in mind as you read the Old Testament references that our definitive sacrifice for all sin has been made by the Lord Jesus Christ. His sacrifice does not erase the need to seek forgiveness, to confess, or to make amends. It does erase the need to offer sacrifices to atone for sin.

What the Word Says

And it shall be, when he is guilty in any of these matters, that he

shall confess that he has sinned in that thing (Lev. 5:5).

Now while I was speaking, praying, and confessing my sin and the sin of my people Israel, and presenting my supplication before the LORD my God for the holy mountain of my God, yes, while I was speaking in prayer, the man Gabriel . . . talked with me, and said, "O Daniel, I have now come forth to give you skill to understand" (Dan. 9:20–22).

[Jesus said,] "If you bring your gift to the altar, and there remember that your brother has something against you, leave your gift there before the altar, and go your way. First be reconciled to your brother, and then come and offer your gift" (Matt. 5:23–24).

Confess your trespasses to one another, and pray for one another, that you may be healed (James 5:16).

What the Word Says to Me

_____

_____

_____

_____

_____

_____

_____

_____

_____

_____

_____

_____

_____

_____

_____

_____

_____

_____

_____

_____

_____

_____

_____

_____

_____

4. Weave this experience into an area of service to others. Use your experience as a foundation stone in helping others. That way, you turn a negative into a positive. When you help others who have sinned in a similar way, or who are in danger of sinning as you have, you become a blessing to others. In no way is this a compensation for your past. Rather, it is an expression that you truly have received God's forgiveness and you are going forward in your life to love and help others. Your witness must not exalt or attempt to exonerate your own past error; it must point others to the saving grace and love of God.

5. Praise God for His generous forgiveness. Our heavenly Father is worthy of our constant praise, and certainly so when it comes to our redemption—our salvation, our ongoing transformation into the likeness of Christ, our spiritual growth and development. We are His children.

Praise is part of *receiving* forgiveness. It is a sign to yourself, to God, and to others that you truly have accepted God's forgiveness and have forgiven yourself.

Praise God, too, when others forgive you. It is an expression of God's forgiveness every time another person forgives you. Accept it as such.

What the Word Says	What the Word Says to Me
Brethren, if anyone among you wanders from the truth, and someone turns him back, let him know that he who turns a sinner from the error of his way will save a soul from death and cover a multitude of sins (James 5:19–20).	
Deliver me from the guilt of bloodshed, O God, The God of my salvation,	

And my tongue shall sing aloud
of Your righteousness.
O Lord, open my lips,
And my mouth shall show forth
Your praise. . . .
The sacrifices of God are a bro-
ken spirit,
A broken and a contrite heart—
These, O God, You will not de-
spise (Ps. 51:14–15, 17).

How Much Will God Forgive?

Can you always count on God's forgiveness? Yes, always. God
will forgive you of your sins committed against Him. God will
forgive you of your trespasses against others; He will strengthen
you and help you as you confess your sin to others and ask their
forgiveness. God will heal you of false guilt and help you to put
completely into the forgiven past the sins of others in which you
were involved.

One day Peter asked Jesus, "Lord, how often shall my brother
sin against me, and I forgive him? Up to seven times?" Jesus
replied, "I do not say to you, up to seven times, but up to seventy
times seven." (See Matt. 18:21–22.)

This number—seventy times seven—refers to an unlimited
perfection of forgiveness. We are to forgive others without end.
Would Jesus ask Peter to do something that God wouldn't do? No.
Our Father holds out unlimited forgiveness to us. We need to
come to Him and receive it.

Does this give a license to sin? No. People who think they can
sin because they can always come to God for forgiveness make a
serious error. In the first place, true believers have no desire to sin.
People who think salvation gives them permission to sin and then
be forgiven repeatedly may not ever have experienced a true
spiritual conversion. In the second place, people who repeatedly
sin and then seek forgiveness develop a hardened heart—a callous

attitude toward their behavior and a cavalier attitude toward God's mercy. Finally, people who sin must face the consequences for the sins. Forgiveness does not erase consequence. The Lord chastises those who sin until they seek and accept forgiveness; the consequences of sin are related to the perfection of God's law. The soul may be cleansed and redeemed, but people reap what they sow in their bodies, relationships, material possessions, and other areas of the natural life.

The Scriptures tell us, "Do not be deceived: 'Evil company corrupts good habits.' Awake to righteousness, and do not sin" (1 Cor. 15:33–34).

- *What new insights do you have into the relationship between sin, guilt, and forgiveness?*

_____

_____

Today Is the Day!

The time has come to be free of guilt! Make today your day to turn to God for forgiveness, to make an appointment with a person you have wronged, to face up to any false guilt weighing you down and keeping you from all that God has for you, and all that God desires to do in you and through you.

If you have never accepted Jesus Christ as your Savior, make today your day of salvation.

Any time you feel a twinge of guilt, turn to the Lord quickly. Face up to your sin, confess it, receive the Lord's forgiveness for it, and leave the incident behind you.

To receive forgiveness is to experience freedom!

LESSON 9

THE ACID OF ANGER

Few people in the Scriptures exhibited as much anger as did King Saul in his jealousy over the blessings of God in David's life. Saul's anger seemed to be triggered when David returned from battle and the women greeted him with this song: "Saul has slain his thousands, and David his ten thousands." The Scriptures tell us, "Saul was very angry, and the saying displeased him" (1 Sam. 18:7–8).

In his anger and jealousy, Saul

- twice threw his spear at David, trying to pin David to the wall (1 Sam. 18:10–11; 19:9–10).
- put David in a position of authority, hoping that David would fail to lead wisely and be discredited (1 Sam. 18:12–15).
- required that David kill one hundred Philistines before he would give him his daughter in marriage, hoping that David would die while fighting the Philistines (1 Sam. 18:25–29).
- pursued David continually for more than a decade, forcing David to live in exile and move frequently from hiding place to hiding place (1 Sam. 24; 26).

Not only did Saul pursue David without mercy, but he ordered the murder of people who helped David. He even turned on his own son with murderous intent. (See 1 Sam. 20:30.) Saul's anger had no end.

It is easy to see anger at work in a person such as Saul. The outbursts are violent, and the rage continues to boil and manifest itself repeatedly over time. The angry person often has visible changes in physical appearance—dilated eyes and tense muscles. Internally, blood pressure rises, and the stomach tends to feel as if it is in knots.

It is far more difficult for us to recognize anger in ourselves. We are such an angry nation as a whole, we tend to tolerate a great deal of anger in our personal lives, families, and neighborhoods. Some even see anger as a sign of strength or power.

This tolerance for anger is contrary to God's Word, and it is damaging to emotional health and well-being. It is also damaging to spiritual growth and witness.

The Scriptures admonish us clearly, "Do not let the sun go down on your wrath, nor give place to the devil" (Eph. 4:26–27). Wrath is linked closely with the work of the evil one in our lives.

- *Can you recall an experience from your past in which you were angry? What did you do? What was the result?*

_____

_____

The Nature and Causes of Anger

Anger is a sudden feeling of displeasure and antagonism in response to an irritating factor. The irritation may be created by a person or a situation. The irritation itself may have been felt for some time, but the response of anger nearly always has an eruption factor. It is not a planned response. The angry person is momentarily out of control—no longer operating according to reason or God's principles of love.

People tend to become angry because

- they aren't allowed to have their own way.
- they are in pain, either physical or emotional.
- they are jealous.

People can become so jealous of other people's possessions, position in life (including relationships), privileges, and personal traits (such as appearance and personality) that they feel others' good fortune somehow spells their own bad fortune.

Intense jealousy and anger manifest themselves in similar ways—with explosive, erratic, sometimes violent, and always irrational overtones. Intensely jealous people are also angry people.

In each example, angry people to some extent feel themselves to be under attack. The attack may be against the will, reputation, status, physical body, marriage, possessions, integrity, or personal sense of well-being.

Sometimes the perceived attack is only a matter of perception. People may see a connection between a current circumstance or behavior and an incident that happened many years ago (for example, abuse as a child). In other instances, people may totally misread others' behavior or motives. The anger that is felt, however, is the same whether the situation that triggered it is real or imagined.

Ultimately, angry people seek to get rid of the perceived or real attacker. King Saul desired to kill David. Violently angry people sometimes resort to physical violence—all forms of which, to some degree, are a prelude to murder. In other cases, they seek to put distance between themselves and the persons causing the irritation.

Anger is usually expressed in one of two ways:

1. *As a physical or verbal outburst.* A person may throw a punch, pound a fist against the wall, slam a door or phone receiver, swear, or shout, among other physical manifestations. Anger may even manifest itself as gossip. Every form of abuse that I can name—sexual, physical, emotional, verbal—has anger at its root.

2. *As a brooding silence.* The person internalizes the anger and allows it to seep into the subconscious. Sometimes this anger displays itself as boredom or an aloofness from other people.

The person who broods in silent anger may manifest an eruption of that anger at a later date. The anger may even erupt within the body in the form of disease. Unless one deals positively and in a godly way with anger, anger will manifest itself in some way.

- *Have you had encounters with people who responded to you with an outburst of anger? How did you feel?*

_____

_____

- *Have you had an encounter with a person who responded to you with brooding silence? How did you feel?*

_____

_____

Nothing good comes from anger, and that is why it is contrary to God's plan for emotional wholeness. Outbursts of anger injure other people. Internalized anger injures the angry person. Both expressions of anger are closely linked to hate. Thus, anger is diametrically opposed to love. When we are angry,

- we cannot respond with sensitivity to the needs of others.
- we lose our ability to feel compassion.
- we cause estrangement.
- we create strife and enmity in relationships.
- we cease to give generously.
- we require unrealistically high standards of behavior from others to compensate for the way we feel we have been injured or attacked.
- we become highly judgmental.

These qualities are certainly not Christlike.

"But what," you may ask, "about the little bursts of anger we all feel from time to time?" People who ask this are usually referring to brief outbursts of anger or daylong pouts. All of these expressions of anger are equally wrong before God. Ask God to forgive you for *all* expressions of anger against other people and to cleanse you of an angry spirit. Then ask the Holy Spirit to fill you with His love, joy, and peace—so that you might manifest these and all the other emotional fruit of the Spirit in your dealings with others.

- *What new insights do you have about anger and its damage to the spiritual life?*

_____

_____

- *In what ways are you feeling challenged about anger?*

_____

_____

Righteous Indignation or Ungodly Anger?

Some people attempt to justify their anger under the banner of righteous indignation. They often point to the behavior of Jesus when He drove the money changers from the temple. They conclude, "I can be angry because Jesus was angry."

Let's look at that incident more closely and in full context:

> Then Jesus went into the temple of God and drove out all those who bought and sold in the temple, and overturned the tables of the money changers and the seats of those who sold doves. And He said to them, "It is written, 'My house shall be called a house of prayer,' but you have made it a 'den of thieves.'" Then the blind and the lame came to Him in the temple, and He healed them (Matt. 21:12–14; see also Mark 11:15–17; Luke 19:45–46).

Mark added in his account that Jesus would not allow anyone to carry wares through the temple (Mark 11:16).

People who have depicted this scene in artwork and in storytelling through the centuries usually show Jesus with whip whirling and eyes blazing as He cleanses the temple. Jesus is given every appearance of being an angry, violent man. That isn't what the Scriptures say. We have no evidence of a physical manifestation of anger from Jesus in any of the gospel accounts that record this story.

The effects of Jesus' actions did overturn the tables of the money changers. Throughout the incident, Jesus' actions were calculated and measured. No riot resulted. Nobody was out of control. Immediately upon the removal of those who were buying and selling, Jesus engaged in a healing service. His righteous indignation was completely without sin and without any diminishing of His spiritual anointing.

We have further evidence for this in the gospel account of Mark, who tells us that earlier that same day, Jesus had looked for figs on a fig tree as He walked from Bethany to Jerusalem. When He found no fruit, Jesus said, "Let no one eat fruit from you ever again"(Mark 11:14).

The next morning after Jesus had cast out the money changers and dove sellers, the disciples noticed that the fig tree had dried up from the roots. When Peter asked about this, Jesus replied,

> Have faith in God. For assuredly, I say to you, whoever says to this mountain, "Be removed and be cast into the sea," and does not doubt in his heart, but believes that those things he says will be done, he will have whatever he says. Therefore I say to you, whatever things you ask when you pray, believe that you receive them, and you will have them. And whenever you stand praying, if you have anything against anyone, forgive him, that your Father in heaven may also forgive you your trespasses. But if you do not forgive, neither will your Father in heaven forgive your trespasses (Mark 11:22–26).

Once you have the full context for what Jesus did in the temple, it is easy to see that:

- Jesus was using the fig tree as a symbol of what was

going to happen to people who were ungodly in their business conduct in the temple. Jesus had in mind when He left Bethany that morning what He was going to do when He arrived at the temple in Jerusalem a few miles away.

- Jesus' emphasis was on prayer and faith during these final days of teaching and healing in the temple. He insisted that His disciples forgive others as a foundation for their prayers being heard. Jesus would not have taught that unless He was approaching those He was about to cast from the temple with a heart filled with forgiveness. His prayers on behalf of "the blind and the lame" would not have been heard otherwise. Only a matter of a few days later, Jesus freely forgave from the cross the people who crucified Him. (See Luke 23:34.) Forgiveness is an act of love, not an expression that flows from anger.

- Jesus taught that His disciples needed only to *speak* to a mountain with faith and it would be cast into the sea. At the time of Jesus' arrest in the Garden, He replied to the man seeking Him, "I am He," and the troops and officers of the chief priests "drew back and fell to the ground." (See John 18:6.) Jesus' words alone held great power. It could very well be that Jesus only spoke to the money changers and dove sellers, and that in their haste to withdraw from Him, they overturned their own tables.

Throughout the scene, Jesus' behavior was

- *without violence.* We have no record of any person being hurt.
- *without resentment.* For example, Jesus did not call upon His disciples to continue the behavior. Nor did He cite any past wrong done to Him as a reason for what He was doing.
- *without bitterness.* Jesus had no heldover feelings

against those who were cast from the temple. He never mentioned them again.

Jesus' action was vented not against the individuals themselves but against their actions, and against the system that allowed buying and selling in God's house of prayer. In every way, Jesus acted in accordance with Psalm 4:4–5:

> *Be angry, and do not sin.*
> *Meditate within your heart on your bed, and be still.*
> *Offer the sacrifices of righteousness,*
> *And put your trust in the LORD. (See also Eph. 4:26.)*

Jesus was indignant or angry in a righteous way. He did not sin in what He did or the way He did it.

Righteous indignation is a healthy response to evil. It is an agitation in the spirit against something that is wrong in God's eyes, without any partiality toward or against the perpetrators of the wrong. The behavior or circumstance is wrong, apart from the personality of any person.

Righteous indignation is expressed in a measured and calculated way. It does not bring physical or emotional harm to another human being. It is thought through in a rational way, and it is behavior that has been preapproved by God through prayer.

Throughout the Scriptures, we are admonished to speak God's truth boldly and to do so in love. I believe that is what Jesus was doing in the temple that day. His words bore great conviction because they were a statement of truth. When we speak the truth boldly, we can expect results, too.

When you take an action or speak the truth with righteous indignation, you must be prepared to reap the consequences that may be associated with the act. Jesus certainly did. The chief priests, scribes, and leaders of the people sought to destroy Jesus after He took this action in the temple. (See Luke 19:47–48.) God stayed their hand until Jesus' ministry among the people was complete, but very soon after, Jesus was arrested, tried, and crucified. Jesus was prepared to die for the good that He had done, including this act of cleansing the temple.

If you truly act in righteous indignation against evil, then you must be prepared to put your life on the line for what you believe and do. The angry person doesn't do this. To the contrary, an angry person tends to act in hopes of destroying the enemy and then to live with a sense of smugness at the victory. The angry person isn't at all interested in suffering or dying for the very person who has done wrong in his eyes.

- *Have you—or do you know a person who has—exhibited words or actions rooted in righteous indignation? What was the result?*

  _____

  _____

- *What new insights do you have into the difference between anger and righteous indignation?*

  _____

  _____

Neutralizing the Acid of Anger

Unchecked anger acts as acid on the soul—eating away at your spirit and eventually destroying all feelings of love toward others. You must neutralize anger as soon as you are aware that you are experiencing it. If you don't, you may very well

- repress it, which is dangerous to you internally, both physically and emotionally.
- suppress it, which is like burying anger alive. It will erupt eventually.
- express it, generally in a way that is hurtful to others.

The alternative God provides for you is to *confess it.*

Confess your anger. Admit to God that you are angry. Ask for His forgiveness, help, and healing.

If you have manifested your anger to another person, go to that person and confess that you have acted in a way contrary to God's plan and desire for your life. Ask the person's forgiveness.

Make certain that your confession to the other person doesn't turn into another bout of confrontation. The point of your confession is not self-justification. Once you have confessed your sin to the person, walk away. Thank God for His forgiveness!

Choose to trust God fully. Anger is one expression that you aren't trusting God fully.

Many people who are angry with others are really angry with God for something they think God has done to them or has failed to do for them. If you are angry with God, you cannot trust God. The cycle is deadly, and the consequences may be eternal; deep anger at God can keep a person out of heaven.

Don't let that happen! Confess your anger to God, and ask Him to forgive you for it. Make a new commitment in your heart and mind to trust God with your entire life, and in following through on that commitment, ask the Holy Spirit daily to lead you, guide you, and protect you from all evil. Also, go to God's Word and read every verse you can find that promises God's sure and ready help to His children.

What the Word Says

"Vengeance is Mine, and recompense;
Their foot shall slip in due time;
For the day of their calamity is at hand,
And the things to come hasten upon them."
For the LORD will judge His people
And have compassion on His servants (Deut. 32:35–36).

What the Word Says to Me

_____

_____

_____

_____

_____

_____

_____

_____

_____

Beloved, do not avenge yourselves, but rather give place to
wrath; for it is written, "Vengeance is Mine, I will repay,"
says the Lord. Therefore
"If your enemy is hungry, feed
him;
If he is thirsty, give him a drink;
For in so doing you will heap
coals of fire on his head."
Do not be overcome by evil, but
overcome evil with good (Rom.
12:19–21).

He who sows iniquity will reap
sorrow,
And the rod of his anger will fail.
He who has a generous eye will
be blessed (Prov. 22:8–9).

- *What new insights do you have into the relationship between anger and emotional health?*

- *In what ways do you feel challenged today to deal with anger?*

THE REPROACH OF REJECTION

Rejection is a form of loneliness; it is estrangement and isolation from others who have not merely forgotten you but also have willfully removed themselves from your presence for some reason. Rejection hurts just as loneliness hurts, but the pain is different. With loneliness, you feel sorrow and sadness that you are alone and separated from desired fellowship. With rejection, the pain is like that of a rusty, dull knife stabbed into the heart. The feeling is one of intense pain accompanied by worthlessness. The rejected person readily concludes, "Nobody loves me; nobody understands me; nobody wants to be around me."

Those who allow rejection to go unchecked tend to transfer their feelings of rejection by one person or group of people to all people. They make a basic assumption that *everybody* is going to reject them. With this attitude, they make themselves less approachable, less likable (since the new acquaintance is made to feel bad for something he hasn't done), and more vulnerable to further rejection.

As with all of the negative emotions discussed in this study guide, the cycle is negative. It can result in

- oversensitivity. Feelings are hurt far too easily.
- bitterness at the person who has rejected him.

- resentfulness, especially toward those she feels are *not* rejected by others.
- suspicions of others. The rejected person may start expecting only bad things in life and, thus, is suspicious of any person who acts in kindness. The rejected person tends to feel he is being set up for a fall by every person he encounters.
- isolation. The rejected person often begins to isolate herself so she won't be hurt by others. She can appear aloof, emotionally distant, or egotistical.
- self-criticalness. The rejected person may put himself down and compare himself unfavorably to others, usually from the motivation that he is going to set himself up for further rejection before the other party can surprise him with rejection.
- guilt—assuming that he is worthy to be rejected.

The rejected person may respond by doing everything in her power to prove to herself and others, "I am someone!" Sometimes this involves changes in appearance, acquisition of status-related possessions, a constant striving for achievement, or perfectionistic behavior.

No two people react to rejection in exactly the same way. The behaviors that manifest rejection, however, are potentially damaging in that they fail to deal with the underlying issue of rejection, and they create situations that require further healing for the person to become emotionally whole. Dealing with rejection is difficult enough without compounding rejection with resentment, bitterness, guilt, egocentric behavior, or a critical spirit.

- *Have you ever felt the pain of rejection? How did you feel? Did you begin to engage in any of the behaviors described above?*

_____

_____

- *Do you know someone who has displayed behaviors stemming from rejection? How did you feel in the person's presence?*

_____

_____

The Nature of Rejection

Rejection nearly always arises from one of two sources:

1. Parents' failure to provide expressions of love.

If a child does not receive needed expressions of love, the child grows up feeling that something is missing or that he was unworthy for some reason of receiving all that he needed.

A child's need for love is just as strong as the basic needs for food and shelter. Children have different capacities for love, and they require love expressed in varying forms. One child may perceive love in terms of abundant hugs and kisses. Another child may feel smothered by hugs and kisses and perceive that a parent is loving if the parent provides a sense of freedom of movement (at the same time staying in close range for protection and approval). Parents must be sensitive to their child's unique personality and need for love.

2. Criticism from others.

Criticism precedes acts of alienation. A person tends to move away from another person because she has drawn a conclusion that being around the other person is undesirable, unhealthful, or dangerous. These are critical evaluations. The rejected person feels not only the isolation when it occurs but also the underlying criticism.

Just as with the root causes of anger, the person feeling rejected may suffer from errors of perception. He may perceive that he has been rejected when the other person wanted some "alone time," or he may perceive that his parents failed to love him fully even though the parents did everything they knew to do to express their love. Perception governs feelings of rejection, however. It doesn't really matter if the rejection was real or imagined. The rejected person feels great pain either way.

Furthermore, the sting of criticism associated with rejection may actually be unwarranted criticism. The person who is doing the rejecting may be suffering from thinking in error or emotional illness. Sometimes a person levels criticism at another person out of insecurity, jealousy, guilt, or weakness. She projects her own failures onto the nearest target and fires critical comments in an attempt to make herself feel better. Once she has registered such intense criticism, rejection follows naturally. It is very difficult for a person who has seriously criticized another to turn around and openly embrace that person as valuable, lovely, desirable, or worthy.

Meanwhile, the rejected person has little recourse. He can do nothing to turn the tide of criticism or to keep the rejection from happening. A feeling of victimization can take over if the rejected person doesn't seek God's healing.

- *Have you had an experience in which one or both of these reasons for rejection occurred?*

- *How did you feel in the wake of rejection?*

Self-Rejection

A third source of rejection is perhaps the most damaging to emotional well-being: self-rejection. The person assumes first that she is worthy of being rejected. Rather than wait for others to reject, the person puts her life into a rejection stance—isolating herself from others, becoming self-critical, seeking self-validation, striving for perfection.

Self-rejection nearly always arises from feelings of guilt associated with sin. The person who commits sin against God or others usually tries to put distance between himself and God or the offended parties.

If you are engaging in this unhealthful emotional response of self-rejection, reread the lesson on guilt. There is something related to sin and forgiveness with which you haven't dealt, or you may be in self-rejection because of false guilt.

You may find it very difficult to recognize that your feelings of rejection are the product of your own behavior. This is something you may need to discuss with a godly counselor who bases advice on God's Word.

- *What new insights do you have into the relationship between rejection and emotional wholeness?*

_____

_____

The Way Out of Rejection

You must do at least six things to recover from feelings of rejection:

1. Recognize the source of the rejection. Identify specifically who you believe has rejected you. If you have vague feelings of rejection, talk to a godly person about them. Your rejection is related to something that someone (or a group of people) has done or said.

As you identify the source of rejection, keep at the forefront of your mind that God never rejects you! He always is available to you with open arms and a heart of love. Apply the truth of the verses below to your life.

What the Word Says	What the Word Says to Me
[Jesus said,] "The one who comes to Me I will by no means cast out" (John 6:37).	_____ _____ _____
And the Spirit and the bride say, "Come!" And let him who hears say, "Come!" And let him who thirsts come. Whoever desires,	_____ _____ _____

let him take the water of life   _____
freely (Rev. 22:17).   _____

[Jesus said,] "Whoever believes   _____
in Him should not perish but   _____
have everlasting life" (John 3:16).   _____

- *Have you ever felt rejected by God? Who really was the source of teaching you this lie (directly or indirectly through example)?*

  _____

  _____

2. Separate the person's rejection of you and the rejection of your deeds. This is especially important if you have been rejected by someone for your witness of Christ or for something good that you did. If love was your motivation, you are in right standing with God.

Some people cannot accept good from others. Their unworthiness causes them to reject those who bless them. In like manner, those who haven't yet accepted Jesus Christ as their Savior and Lord find it difficult to accept fully those who are Christians. The person isn't rejecting you solely; he is also rejecting God.

In cases where you know you have done something bad and the rejection of others is a response to your behavior, own up to what you have done. Confess your wrong to God and to others. Seek to make amends when possible. Accept God's forgiveness, and make a new commitment to better behavior. At no time, however, should you draw a conclusion that you are a bad person who can never be redeemed, saved, or forgiven. Never conclude that you have no value or worth.

To God, you are always of infinite value and worth. God's love for you has no bounds. You may have acted in a sinful way—you may even be a sinner, with sin as the state of your soul—but you are not beyond God's ability to forgive you. Admit what you are feeling, and receive God's forgiveness.

3. Reject the rejection. In the final analysis, only God's opinion of you counts. He never rejects you. Once you are forgiven by God, you stand in a cleansed state before Him. No amount of dirt that others throw at you in the form of criticism should be allowed to stick to you. In the face of criticism and rejection, you need to proclaim with boldness to your spirit, "I am accepted, loved, and forgiven by God, and His response is all that matters."

Read these encouraging words from Paul's letter to the Ephesians:

> [I] do not cease to give thanks for you, making mention of you in my prayers: that the God of our Lord Jesus Christ, the Father of glory, may give to you the spirit of wisdom and revelation in the knowledge of Him, the eyes of your understanding being enlightened; that you may know what is the hope of His calling, what are the riches of the glory of His inheritance in the saints, and what is the exceeding greatness of His power toward us who believe (Eph. 1:16–19).

Paul says that he desires for these Christians in Ephesus to know these things. And we are to know these things in our lives today:

The hope of God's calling. God desires for you *not* to be isolated or filled with feelings of rejection; rather, He desires that you might have hope for the future—that you will enjoy deep and abiding friendships with other Christians whom the Lord is preparing to bring into your life so that together, you and your new friends, associates, or coworkers might fulfill God's plan on this earth. God designed His church to function as a body, and that means God has a role and function for you to fulfill. His purpose for you is not rejection, but fulfillment in loving relationships with other Christians.

The riches of the glory of His inheritance. There is no eternal blessing that God desires to withhold from any person who proclaims Jesus as Lord.

The exceeding greatness of His power. Trust God to deal with the person who has rejected you falsely—to enlighten him in his error, to convict him of his criticism, to move upon his heart so he might treat you with kindness in the future. God is able and willing to do this. Ask Him to work on your behalf so that all things in your life will come to a good and fruitful end.

- *What new insights do you have into the healing God desires for rejection?*

_____

_____

4. Forgive the person who has rejected you. You need to identify the person who caused your feelings of rejection (step 1) so that you may forgive that person. You must also forgive any person who has erroneously taught you that God may have rejected you.

Forgiveness does not mean that the person's behavior was right, or that it didn't hurt. No, forgiveness means letting the offending party go. In forgiving, you are freeing the offending person from your heart and entrusting the person to God. In freeing her, you are free *of* her and of her hurtful influence. The person is never free, however, from God's watchful eye and from what God will require of her.

- *Have you ever forgiven someone who wronged you or rejected you? How did you feel when you did this? What was the result in your life?*

_____

_____

5. Put your full focus on God. Concentrate on who God is in your life. He is your Creator, Savior, daily Comforter, and Counselor. He knows everything about you and loves you unconditionally. He can move heaven and earth on your behalf. He is always present and available to you. And He will never reject you or disown you.

Even if the entire world seems to reject you, God does not. Invest in the one relationship in your life that will never be marred by rejection. Spend time with God. Pour out your devotion toward Him. He will bring into your life others who can receive your talents and gifts, love you deeply, and delight in your unique personality.

Immerse yourself in God's Word so that you can understand more fully the almighty God and heavenly Father who is the eternal lover of your soul. Stay in close fellowship with Him.

6. *Give generously to others.* The person who freely and generously gives to others—of time, presence (more than presents), attention, genuine compliments, a listening ear—is rarely rejected. Turn outward from your rejection to embrace life and to reach out to other people.

As you read through the verses below, note God's repeated desire to work in you and through you. He longs to have a relationship with you.

What the Word Says	What the Word Says to Me
That you, being rooted and grounded in love, may be able to comprehend with all the saints what is the width and length and depth and height—to know the love of Christ which passes knowledge; that you may be filled with all the fullness of God (Eph. 3:17–19).	
Now may the God of peace Himself sanctify you completely; and may your whole spirit, soul, and body be preserved blameless at the coming of our Lord Jesus Christ. He who calls you is faithful, who also will do it (1 Thess. 5:23–24).	
That which we have seen and	

heard we declare to you, that you
also may have fellowship with us;
and truly our fellowship is with
the Father and with His Son Jesus Christ. And these things we
write to you that your joy may be
full (1 John 1:3–4).

[Jesus said,] "Freely you have received, freely give" (Matt. 10:8).

_____
_____
_____
_____
_____
_____
_____

_____
_____

God's desire for you is not that you feel the anguish and reproach of rejection, but that you experience His love and that you enjoy the fellowship and friendship of others who follow His Son, Jesus Christ.

For you truly to be healed of the effects of rejection in your life—and to keep this damaging emotion from alienating you from others—you must choose to allow God's love to enter your heart. Open up your life today to Him. Invite Him to do His deep, inner healing work in you.

MY FINAL WORD TO YOU

One statement sums up all that God desires to do in your life so that your emotions might be sound, positive, and beneficial: God desires to *heal* your emotions and make you whole.

One word sums up the means that God uses to heal you: *love.*

When your self-esteem is based on the work of a loving heavenly Father, a redeeming Savior, Christ Jesus, and a divine Counselor and Comforter, the Holy Spirit; when you stand forgiven before the Father; when you have made a decision to be free of the ache of anxiety, the grip of fear, the grindstone of guilt, the acid of anger, and the reproach of rejection—you have chosen to receive God's love.

God's love is extended to you in many forms, including forgiveness. His presence in you is always a loving presence. His work through you is always a work of love toward others.

Nothing is more attractive than love. Nothing is more beneficial to your emotional well-being. Nothing is more potent in making you emotionally whole. Nothing gives a greater lift to life.

But God's love isn't automatically experienced by everyone. It is freely made available to all people, but individually, you must choose to receive His love. It is the fountain from which emotional wholeness flows!